MY
SIXTEEN

MY
SIXTEEN

A Self-Help Guide to Finding *Your* Sixteen Great-Great-Grandparents

Robert W. Marlin

Land Yacht Press

Nashville

Published
by
Land Yacht Press
Nashville, Tennessee

Copyright © 1996 by Robert W. Marlin
All Rights Reserved

Printed on acid-free paper
in the United States of America

First printing, July 1996

Cover design by Go Design, LLC
Interior design by C. Sutherland
Edited by Deborah Wiseman

ISBN 0-9650513-0-7

Land Yacht Press is an imprint of the

Richiuso Publishing Group

To order multiple copies of *My Sixteen* write or fax:
Land Yacht Press
P.O. Box 210262
Nashville, TN 37221-0262
FAX: 615-646-2086

Several years ago I received a response to a query letter regarding the publication of this book. A gentleman advised me that his organization did not publish books on this subject. He did add that he would be happy to read sample chapters and perhaps make a suggestion as to who I might contact.

His response to my writing was positive and encouraging. We kept in touch periodically, and I did follow up on several of his suggestions. His continuing positive attitude, good nature, and natural enthusiasm never failed to give me a lift. Neither of us had any idea at the time that he would eventually be the publisher of this book. So, it is with heart felt appreciation and thanks that I dedicate this book to John-Paul (Jay) Richiuso of Land Yacht Press.

Contents

Prologue   9

Chapter 1: My Search Begins   13

Chapter 2: Talks with My Mother
            and Research Etiquette   31

Chapter 3: Family Research Resumes   53

Chapter 4: My Mother's Story Continues   77

Chapter 5: Marlin's Census Without
            the Soundex Method   105

Chapter 6: Declaration of Intention for
            Naturalization   129

Chapter 7: 1920 Federal Census   153

Chapter 8: Primary Sources   171

Chapter 9: Computer Genealogy   207

Epilogue   213

Appendix: Suggested Reading and
            Reference Material
            Genealogical Computer
            Programs   217

Index   225

Prologue

Sometime in the late fall of 1936, at the age of six, I obtained my first library card. The only requirement was the ability to sign my own name. I can only assume that someone in the educational or library system thought that this qualification might be a great incentive to get kids interested in their own educational development. I had learned to write my name just weeks earlier, when the fall school term had started.

On that first Monday after Labor Day, I entered the world of the first grade. On the desk in front of each student was a card approximately two inches high and about ten inches long. Each student's name was penned in ink in beautiful script on one of these cards. Our teacher, Miss Connelly, introduced herself and then gave a short talk on the value of being able to write one's own name. She pointed out that this was the only prerequisite to obtaining a library card. No more encouragement was needed for me. Within the month I was able to pen my own name.

The ability did not come easily. It required everyday practice. This practice was followed by a daily critical analysis from Miss Connelly, who pointed out everything that was wrong with our efforts. I was one of the first to master the skill. Many of the other kids did not acquire this same skill until the end of the school term and some never really acquired it at all. However, there was a direct relationship between the amount of effort expended and the degree of skill eventually attained. This type of challenge faced by children

of the thirties still exists for people today. How well you succeed at anything is directly related to how much effort you
are willing to expend.

Today, I serve on the board of directors of the Jewish Genealogical Society of Greater Orlando. I am also a member
of their Mentors Group, which offers special help and advice
to newer members. I constantly hear complaints and laments
from members and other researchers about their inability to
locate genealogical information. In some cases, I am able to
locate the information in less than thirty minutes. Sometimes
it is only necessary to point out a source that was there all
the time but hadn't been checked. In either case, the people
involved hadn't made the effort to do their own homework.
It occurred to me that some things had not changed in more
than fifty years.

When I first became involved in genealogical research in
1977, only about five or six books on the subject existed.
What I found was more than enough to get me started; however, as I progressed and looked for more books, they simply did not exist. After reading what was available, my research continued using the trial and error method. This
simply means that I tried method after method until I found
the right one. It was time consuming and sometimes tedious,
but over a period of time I have developed methods that
work for me.

At this time there are dozens of books available that cover
many areas of research. There is something to be learned in
every one of them. I constantly hear researchers say that
they don't have the time for reading. To hear adults say this
always astounds me. Few of them realize that just breezing
through some of this bonanza couldn't help but increase
their genealogical yield.

This book is designed to take you through, step-by-step,
exactly what I have experienced and learned over the years.

It will also show you how to attain similar results. It will point out the joys as well as the pitfalls encountered in genealogical research. It will not tell you where to write for a birth certificate, but it will explain what information you can expect to find on a birth certificate, as well as how to take the information supplied and use it to find more information. It is not presented in a concise, well ordered-manner, simply because genealogical research is seldom pursued, or information uncovered, in a concise, well-ordered manner. This does not mean that my approach is not organized or efficient; just the opposite. I want you to uncover the most information with the least amount of wasted effort. In this field of endeavor the final result is what is most important. The end result I am trying to help you achieve is an accurate, well-documented, and authentic genealogical chart.

Many people helped and contributed time as well as documents that went into the preparation of this book. The single biggest contributor was my wife, Sylvia. She contributed countless hours of her time to make sure that I never became discouraged or felt alone. We have been married for almost twenty years, but I still refer to her and think of her as my bride. It is her never ending support, ideas for improvement, and belief in me that make everything else worthwhile.

A note of thanks to Ms. Eleanor Crawford and the staff at the Genealogy Department of the Orlando Public Library. Her attention to detail makes every genealogist's job a little easier. My gratitude also to each and every one of the gracious ladies at the Family History Center at the Latter Day Saints Church in Lake Mary, Florida. Their dedication, willingness to assist, and never ending patience should be an inspiration to all who use their facilities.

My special thanks go out to three of my newfound cousins. The first is Vivian Myerson who first introduced me to a real-life "Aunt Jenny." Also Ruth Resnick of Oceanside, California. Ruth was an endless supply of information and help in verifying numerous facts. And last but not least, a very special thanks to Leslie Margolin Auerbach of Eugene, Oregon, with whom I share a special relationship in spite of the fact that we have never met. Not only do we share a common grandfather, but more important, we each supplied a missing link in the life of the other. Without all three I could never have come this far.

CHAPTER 1

My Search Begins

It has been said that we all give some thought to divine Providence when seemingly chance events occur that change our lives forever. Such an event occurred to me on my mother's seventieth birthday. Several of my nieces and nephews had called to wish Grandma a happy birthday. Quite suddenly I realized that I had no idea who my own grandparents were. It further occurred to me at that moment that I had spent my entire life totally unaware that grandparents existed.

As a direct result of that chance realization, which occurred more than eighteen years ago, my life was changed forever. Since then, I have come to know all four of my grandparents. I've also come to know all eight of my great-grandparents as well as seven of my sixteen great-great-grandparents. And the search goes on. . . . Unfortunately, I never got to know any of them while they were still alive. However, finding them now is no less exciting.

The men engaged in various occupations. There was a wine-maker, a cabinetmaker, a rabbi, a clerk, and a ship's carpenter, just to name a few. The women all had one common trait. They all bore large numbers of offspring, many of whom did not survive the first ten years of life. Some came to America as early as 1848, while others arrived as late as 1906. They came from France, Germany, Denmark, and Russia and they included Catholics, Protestants, and Ashkenazic Jews.

Also as a result of my chance event, I have traveled thousands of miles for research and information. There have been trips to Boston, Washington, D.C., Jacksonville, Buffalo, Trenton, Bayonne, and Philadelphia. During the next three years I hope to visit Alsace, Baden, Copenhagen, Kiev, Bobruisk, Minsk, and Israel. Additionally as a direct result of that evening, I have become a competent amateur photographer as well as a serious historian and geographer. I've studied American history, eighteenth and nineteenth century European history and geography, and the turn-of-the century flight and Diaspora of Eastern European Jews. My studies have also included the political geography of these countries.

We all carry the surname as a supreme tribute to the male ego. In reality, we could carry the surname of any of our other forebears with equal dignity and historical accuracy. From a genetic standpoint, there is no favoritism given to the male partner. Here, the female of the species can overcome male chauvinism. Genetically, there is usually some of each of them in each of us. However, there can be more of one side than the other. Perhaps this is why some of us feel closer to one side of the family than the other, without realizing why. The very act of seeking out my ancestors has added a dimension to my life that has been sorely missing. However, this is only part of the story I am attempting to relate.

My parents had gone through a bitter divorce when I was a child. My mother had never met my father's family and therefore knew nothing about his ethnic or family background. So much for my paternal grandparents. My maternal grandmother had died fifteen years before I was born, and my mother was totally estranged from her father. So much for maternal grandparents. As a child, I can't remember giving the matter much thought. Looking back now, I realize that it was probably some sort of defense mechanism to stop the hurt in situations such as when other kids bragged about what their grandparents had given them for Christmas or for their birthday.

I didn't see my father until I was in the military on my way to Korea. We then saw each other infrequently for several years. However, at no time would he allow discussion of any aspect of his background or early life as a child or young man. He did, however, slip once and mention that he had a brother named Paul, who was on the police force and lived in Maspeth, which is a section of Queens, in New York City. He had mentioned that he had visited Paul several months after the bombing of Pearl Harbor, at the start of World War II. My father died in California in 1966. At various times I had an idle curiosity regarding his background. However, it was not strong enough for me to pursue the matter.

While visiting my mother several weeks after her seventieth birthday, I casually asked if she knew the first names of my father's parents. At that particular moment my question must have jarred a long forgotten memory because she came forth with a story I could not believe. When I was born in 1931, my father had wanted to name me after his father, who had died several years earlier. When my mother found out that his name had been Meyer, she would have no part of that. It sounded too Jewish. They later compromised on Robert. I'm certain that my father was aware, and my mother doesn't know to this day, that Robert is one of the many Hebrew transliterations of the name Meyer. My

mother also seemed to recall that his mother's name may
have been Hilda, but she was not certain. In any case, it was
at this time that my life was changed forever.

The following day I started out on what was to become
my own age of discovery. Armed with several names, one
location, and not really having any idea of where to start, I
began my search. My first stop was at what had been my
very own information center since I was ten, the New York
Public Library. I went on a hunt for old telephone books,
and found them on microfilm. Aside from the names of my
grandparents, I also knew that my father had visited his
brother Paul in 1942. The simple act of filling out a slip of
paper brought me a reel of microfilm that contained the
Queens telephone directory for that year. My first attempt to
use the microfilm reader was almost a disaster, but within
five minutes I was going at Mach 4. Success was almost immediate. There it was:

Margolin, Paul
58-81 57th Maspeth Evergreen 9016

In my mind at that time, it was akin to discovering America. When I settled down, I realized that the only thing I had
really discovered was that I had an uncle named Paul who
had lived in Maspeth forty-five years earlier. None of the
other entries of the same surname meant anything to me.
Feeling somewhat disappointed, I returned the roll of film.
The young lady at the desk must have sensed my disappointment and asked if she could help. I briefly explained
what I was looking for. She immediately suggested that I try
the old city directories, which were the forerunners of telephone books. They listed people by name, address, and occupation. They also sometimes included the name of the

1933/34 Brooklyn–Queens City Directory.

spouse of the person listed. The latest one available was the 1933—1934 Brooklyn-Queens edition. I filled out another slip and within five minutes had hit pay dirt again. The words almost literally jumped out of the page and hit me between the eyes. Under the name Margolin was listed:

Margolin, Hilda (widow Meyer)
370 E. 54th Brooklyn

There were dozens of entries for persons with the surname Margolin. Scanning the remainder I also found:

Margolin, Paul	Policeman	370 E. 54th
Margolin, Ruth	Clerk	370 E. 54th
Margolin, Samuel	Bookkeeper	370 E. 54th
Margolin, William	Chauffeur	370 E. 54th

All were listed at the same address as my grandmother
Hilda.

Not only was my uncle Paul listed, but so was my father,
William, who at that time was in the U.S. Navy and drove a
limousine for an admiral. I hadn't experienced this kind of
excitement in years. Here in one day I had found a set of
grandparents, a father and an uncle, plus an uncle and an
aunt I hadn't even known about. I had found an entire family. Lots of questions immediately started to enter my mind.
Was my grandmother still alive? Should I try to contact her?
How about the others? Should I try to contact anyone?
Where do I go from here? Within minutes my mind was totally bogged down from trying to analyze all the potential
possibilities. Feeling somewhat less exhilarated, I returned
the microfilm to the desk and left. It was quite obvious my
next step would require some advance planning.

Early the next morning, I was standing at the front door
of my local library in Great Neck, Long Island, at opening
time. A quick search for any books on ancestor hunting produced four volumes, which I promptly checked out. I spent
the next two days devouring them. The best one I found
was entitled, *Finding Your Roots*, by Jeanne Eddy Westin

(see Appendix). It was to become my temporary bible on genealogy, and was the start of my education in that field.

Several days later, I was trying to tear down the massive steel doors at the New York Public Library. It was only 9:45 A.M. and those doors did not open until 10:00. I was the first one through the door when it opened, and I raced to the third floor where the Genealogy Department was located. After signing in and filling out the usual paper slip I sat at a numbered table, my mind racing, while I waited for several volumes of death indexes to be brought to me. If Hilda was a widow in 1933, it was only necessary to work backward from then in order to locate the death certificate of my grandfather Meyer. Less than twenty minutes later I had what I was looking for:

Margolin, Meyer 15 July 1930 Brooklyn #14771

It seemed almost too easy. After copying down the information necessary to apply for a death certificate, I took the subway downtown and went directly to the Vital Records Division of the Department of Health. After filling out an application and paying the proper fee I was informed that the certificate would arrive by mail in about two weeks. From there I walked to the city clerk's office to try to find a marriage license for my grandparents. All of this new-found methodology had been found in the books I had read.

My father had been born sometime around 1910. Once again, it was a matter of going backward from that year. It only took a six-year search of the index to find what I was looking for. After filling out still another form and paying the proper fee I was again advised that the certificate would arrive by mail in about two weeks. Official responses to my requests were beginning to sound like a broken record.

For the next two weeks I read everything I could find on the subject of genealogy, roots, and ancestor hunting. The marriage license arrived on the thirteenth day. I had been haunting the mailbox and almost kissed the mailman. The license was loaded with information. My grandfather was the son of Hirsch Margolin and Temma Kranz. My grandmother's maiden name was Koris, and she was the daughter of Hyman Koris and Pessie Budiansky. It also listed their home addresses, the name of the rabbi who married them, and the names of the witnesses.

It was hard to believe that just one piece of paper had taken me back to the fourth generation of my father's family. The death certificate arrived the next day. It contained a wealth of information, but little of it was in agreement with the information contained in the marriage license. The names of the wife and parents were different and so was the age at time of death. This experience provided me with my first disappointment, as well as my first lesson in the importance of accuracy and documentation. It quickly became quite obvious that I had a death certificate for the wrong Meyer Margolin. A trip back to the library confirmed everything. By going back an additional two years in the index I found another entry:

Margolin, Meyer 28 December 1928 Queens #7624

It was necessary to wait another two weeks for the death certificate to arrive. It proved to be the right one. The most important piece of information I wanted was at the bottom of the certificate:

PLACE OF BURIAL: MONTEFIORE CEMETERY SPRINGFIELD GDNS, N.Y.

THE CITY OF NEW YORK

C 22848 OFFICE OF THE CITY CLERK rk No.HD 2542   04

Marriage Register

MARRIAGE LICENSE BUREAU—BOROUGH OF MANHATTAN

Certificate of Marriage Registration

This Is To Certify That Meyer Margolin

residing at 141 Monroe St.   born (Age 25 years

at Russia   and ˙Hilda Koris

residing at 368 E 4th St.   born (Age 22 years

at Russia

Were Married

on January 8 1904   at   New York NY

1st marriage for both parties

grooms parents-Hirsch   Temma Kranz

brides parents-Hyman   Pessie Budiansky

as shown by the duly registered license and certificate of marriage of said persons on file in this office.

THIS CERTIFICATE IS VOID IF ALTERED

FACSIMILE SIGNATURE AND SEAL
ARE PRINTED PURSUANT TO SECTION 11-A,
DOMESTIC RELATIONS LAW OF NEW YORK

Dated at the Municipal Building, Manhattan

May 8   79
_____ 19____

DAVID N. DINKINS
City Clerk of the City of New York

RF 447-20M sets-718022-X77(78) 346

Transcript of Marriage Licence of Meyer Margolin and Hilda Korris.

Sleep that night was next to impossible as my mind once again bogged down with the possibilities of what I might find the next day. I was up at dawn even though I knew the cemetery didn't open until 9:00 A.M.

It was only a fifteen-minute ride on the Cross Island Expressway from Northern Boulevard to the Springfield Boulevard exit. Five minutes later I arrived at my destination. The stone building that served as an entryway to the cemetery looked like a medieval fortress. The large plaque read simply: Montefiore Cemetery. The telephone instruction had seemed simple enough. Follow Montefiore Road through

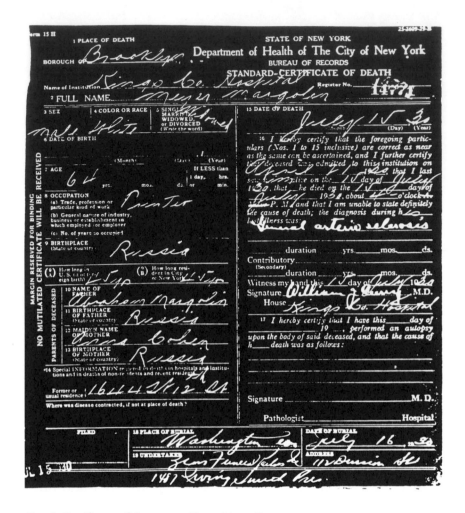

Death Certificate of the wrong Meyer Margolin.

the middle of the cemetery to North 9th Street. Turn left, go to Abraham Avenue, and turn right. Then I was to look for a gate marked, "United Friends and Relatives," which was the name of the Jewish burial society where my grandfather was buried. Afraid that I would pass it in spite of my turtle-like pace, I decided to park the car and walk. About two hundred feet farther along I found the right entryway and walked directly through it, right into my past.

Death Certificate of Meyer Margolin.

As I proceeded, my eyes came directly in contact with a large headstone with the word *Meyer* distinctly visible above the overgrown yews. This had to be it. I approached the grave site, pushed the yews aside and read the English part of the inscription:

Entrance to the Jewish Burial Society named, "United Friends and Relatives."

Meyer Margolin
Died December 28, 1928

At this point I couldn't control the flow of tears and my mouth involuntarily uttered the word, "Grampa." I couldn't remember crying before as a grown man, but at this point I was unable to control the flow of tears.

After regaining my composure I began reading some of the other headstones. Several rows away I found what I was looking for. It was a stone with an open book carved upon its surface. On one side of the book the initials H. M. were also engraved. As I parted the overgrown yews I could once again read the English portion of the inscription:

Headstone at gravesite of Hilda Margolin.   *Headstone at gravesite of Meyer Margolin.*

Hilda Margolin
Died January 26, 1962

My grandmother, whom I had never even known, was also gone. It is impossible to fully describe the feelings I experienced during those moments. They were a combination of euphoria, happiness, sadness, and depression, all at the same time. However, for the first time in my life I felt an awareness of continuity with my past. That feeling is still strong and vibrant after all these years.

For more than two weeks after my visit to the cemetery, I did little more than think about, and attempt to analyze, just exactly what I had uncovered. Probably the single most significant, indisputable fact was that there was virtually no doubt that I now had two fully Jewish grandparents. This alone made me immediately and totally aware that no matter what I may have thought before, I was now half Jewish, and would be for the remainder of this lifetime. In spite of my mother's lifelong insistence that the surname Margolin was not Jewish, I also became painfully aware that if I had been born in Germany in 1931 instead of America, the chances were good that I would probably have become just another statistic of the Holocaust. Almost fifty years of denial now had to be dealt with and overcome. At that time I had no idea of the far-reaching effects this small amount of research and new knowledge was going to have upon my long-term future. What had started out weeks earlier as an experiment in idle curiosity had already changed my life forever. The most startling thing to me then was something that was not readily discernible, and had to do with my childhood background. It is not the most commonplace thing for a person with a Jewish sounding surname, who was reared as an Episcopal in a Catholic neighborhood that was notably anti-Semitic, to suddenly discover that he is really half Jewish.

In school, I'm certain that the majority of us found the study of world history boring and extremely difficult to relate to. The French satirist, historian, and philospher Voltaire is credited with stating, "History is fables agreed upon." In 1917, Henry Ford was quoted in the *Chicago Tribune* as saying, "History is more or less bunk." In my opinion both men were right. Perhaps that is because in conflict, war, or politics, most world history is written only from the viewpoint of the winner. When studied closely, most of the great men and women of history are not nearly as glamorous as reported. It is possible to get a much closer prospective of world history by studying genealogy. In reality, the study of genealogy is nothing more than a study of world history on a totally personal basis. However, the cast of characters is your own ancestors. Is there any doubt that what they did a hundred or a thousand years ago has had some direct effect on the quality and outcome of your life? Is there any doubt that each of these people made some small contribution to the outcome of world history? Uncovering what part your ancestors played in the drama of world history is what genealogy is all about.

Almost all societies place a totally unwarranted importance on the male family surname, some almost to the point of mysticism. No doubt, this is probably the result of several thousand years of male world rule. Because of this, many people doing genealogical research work only on their own surname, ignoring everything else along the way. This to me represents the ultimate ego trip, and does little to add anything to your life or well-being. Others trace only descendants on the paternal side, once again attaching some mystique to the male. This is especially strange for Jews inasmuch as most Orthodox Jews insist that in order to be a Jew, one must have a Jewish mother. After that, the surname appears to be somewhat unimportant to them. The end result of this type of archaic thinking exists in almost all phases of genealogical study. Even the material you are forced to work with contains centuries of male-dominated methods of record keeping.

When it comes to your ancestral chart, this type of problem plays only as large a part as you allow it to. In my genealogical chart each of the individuals entered shares equal billing and equal importance. It doesn't take long to realize that genealogical research and computers share an important concept. They both operate on basic principles of binary mathematics. In other words, each time you go one step forward, the number of items doubles.

For example: Each of us has
2   Parents
4   Grandparents
8   Great-grandparents
16   Great-great-grandparents
         Etc., etc., etc.

This list adds up to only thirty-one individuals, including you. It represents five generations, which can sometimes cover as little as one hundred years in time. However, in each individual case in this small pyramid, it is safe to say that if any one of the individuals had not been in the right place at the right time, the reader would not be around to read these words, nor would I have been around to write them. Keep in mind that these are *direct* descendants and do not include any sisters, brothers, cousins, uncles, or aunts. The mathematics of genealogy is truly mind boggling.

Aside from any historical importance our ancestors may have played in influencing world history, there are numerous other factors to consider. For example, each of us is composed of millions of body cells. Each of these cells contains a nucleus, which with certain exceptions, contains forty-six chromosomes. Half of these chromosomes are transmitted to us by each of our parents. The chromosomes in turn contain the genes that predetermine hundreds of factors that influence our lives. They determine how tall we will be, the size of our body, the color of our eyes and hair, our facial features, personality traits, and hundreds of other factors that will ultimately influence our lives and destinies. Each year new scientific research discovers new gene-influenced factors.

However, parents only play the role of messenger in your genetic makeup. The actual genes passed on come from your four grandparents and the distribution of the genes you receive is a total mathematical crapshoot. The distribution is seldom even or equal in any way. This is what makes each one of us a totally unique human being.

From a medical standpoint it can be extremely important to know something about your biological background. Almost every ethnic group on this planet is prone to diseases that are unique to that group. Just as African Americans are excessively prone to contracting sickle cell anemia, Eastern European Jews are subject to contracting Tay-Sachs disease, a genetically inherited disease that destroys the central nervous system. It is important to remember that biology seldom recognizes male dominance and seldom recognizes male chauvinism. Any of your positive inherited traits can just as easily come from a maternal line. The point is that knowing who you are and where you came from can be important for reasons other than pure ego.

My business life and social life were almost nonexistent during this period. I fell asleep at night thinking about what I was going to study or research the next day. Most of my time was spent reading everything I could locate relating to genealogy. In this short period of time I became almost obsessed with finding out more about who I really was and from "whence I had come." It quickly became apparent that if I continued my research the chances were good that I would uncover other things, which I had better be prepared to accept. Those fifty years of denial would probably have to be dealt with much faster than I might have wanted to. In addition, I was not aware that I had two uncles and one aunt who were probably still alive. Should I try to find them? Would they care to meet me? Did they even know that I existed? Did I have cousins? All of these and dozens of other questions popped into my mind as I tried to get my thoughts organized. In retrospect, I realize that being organized and proceeding with caution is the only way to approach what I call constructive genealogical research.

If there is a single truth in genealogical research, it is that nobody agrees on anything. There is no right or wrong way to approach the subject. No hard-and-fast rules—only numerous guidelines. This applies to obtaining information as well as recording it. During my earliest period I did realize that it would be necessary to set a realistic goal of what I wanted to accomplish, and then reach that goal before proceeding farther.

The main truth I discovered and learned from all of my reading was that if you truly want to succeed in genealogical research, then you must come prepared to do your lessons and then do your own homework. In other words, you must be prepared to do the work yourself and not depend on others. In most research facilities, the librarians are there to guide you to the information. It is not their job to look it up for you. You must be prepared to spend as much time as necessary to find what you are looking for. If patience is not one of your virtues, then I strongly suggest that you pursue some other endeavor. For example, when you are seeking a marriage, birth, or death certificate you must discover how the name was spelled at the time the information was recorded. Was the first name "Catherine" spelled with a *C* or a *K*? Was the surname "Brown" originally spelled "Broune"? When looking at indexes you must be prepared to spend as much time as necessary to check every possible variation in the spelling of a name. If you depend on someone else to look up the information they will usually check only the spelling you supply them with. Some of the more common surnames can have dozens of spelling variations.

The hardest part in getting started is choosing a direction and then deciding exactly what you want to accomplish. In my opinion the bottom line seems to be that dedication and attention to detail will ultimately mean the difference between failure and success.

CHAPTER 2

Talks with My Mother and Research Etiquette

During this early period, I never told my mother about the research I had already done on my father's family. From the beginning it was apparent that she tacitly disapproved of my curiosity. When it came to any additional information about my father's family, it was quite clear that I had already received all I was going to get from my mother. Any additional inquiries were met with, "I don't remember," or "I never knew." If I pressed for more details about my father's family, she slowly became less and less responsive.

It was much easier for her to talk about her own family and childhood. For the first time in my life we began to have talks about her childhood in turn-of-the-century Brooklyn. The first meeting went on for more than two hours. After that, we met at least once a week. At times she was actually eager to relate all the minute details of what sometimes seemed a totally mundane incident. However, I never interrupted her once she had started. Under no circumstances would she allow me to tape-record the conversations.

My mother was born Florence Helena Kruse in January of 1907. She was the oldest daughter of John Patrick Kruse and Catherine Wild. Both of her parents were born in the 1880s and were almost the same age. Mother had two sisters, Marian and Catherine, and a brother, John Jr. Her mother had died in 1916 when she was only nine years old. John Sr. had been born in Brooklyn; the elder Catherine in Boston. The Wild family had moved from Boston to Brooklyn immediately after the Great Blizzard of 1888. Mother remembered that when she was a child, sometime before she started school, her father had worked as a driver for a lumber company. The wagon was pulled by a pair of horses named John and Katie. John came home for lunch every day and parked the team in front of their house at 20 Oakland Street. All the kids who lived on their street looked forward to this daily event. John Sr. had a brother named Fred who was killed in a traffic accident. He had been driving a horse-drawn hearse that was hit by either a train or trolley car. John Sr. also had a much older sister named Lena, who was married to a man named John Johnson, and they lived right down the street from the Kruses. Little more was known about the family of John Sr., except that his family had lived there as far back as anyone could remember. However, after thinking about it for a few minutes, my mother recalled that on several occasions Lena had mentioned that as a young girl she had lived in Manhattan.

If John Sr. had any early religious training, my mother was not aware of it. Catherine was a practicing Catholic and all of the children were baptized as Catholics. When Catherine died, all four children were then cared for and later raised by John Sr's. housekeeper and mistress, Clara Halloran, who later came to be known to me as Nana. Some years later, after a falling out with her, my grandfather moved out and never returned. John Sr. periodically supported and visited the children for years. However, all custody and care was left to his ex-mistress. Clara must have made life for the kids a living hell a good part of the time. There was so much bitterness expressed by my mother during the telling of this part of her story that it is difficult to separate fact from fiction. That is part of your job as a genealogist and family historian.

My mother's father later remarried after "taking up" with a young girl not much older than my mother. Her name was Georgetta. They had three children, but only one survived. This was my mother's half brother, Kenneth. Georgetta died sometime shortly after having the third child, leaving my grandfather with a child to raise by himself. To some it must have seemed like some form of poetic justice, considering how he had avoided raising his other four children. Kenneth was born a year after I was born, creating a situation where a nephew is older than his uncle. John Sr. died in 1956. Further research showed that he died less than a mile from where he had been born.

This first session with my mother ended before we had even gotten to her mother's family. In passing, she mentioned that her grandfather Wild fled France in 1870 to avoid military service in the German Army. I was already intrigued and could hardly wait to find out more about a great-grandfather who was a draft-dodger. In any case, I now had all the information necessary to begin a genealogical search on my mother's side of the family.

During this period of my research, I became aware that even this type of information gathering was a learning process not to be taken lightly. In the process of conducting an oral interview, above all else, you want the person you are talking with to voluntarily give you facts that are not clouded or jaded by their own egocentricity. My own mother, under the best of circumstances, was not an easy person to interview or one to provide straightforward answers. Her unhappy childhood was filled with events that left her resentful and bitter. As a result, the details regarding her own family were sketchy and sometimes inaccurate.

The first thing I did was to send for the death certificates of both maternal grandparents. By now I was slowly becoming an expert in the art of patiently waiting. No matter how long it might take for the ordered documents to arrive, I would simply go on to other aspects of research or genealogical study while waiting. When these death certificates arrived, the data contained in them started me on another adventure that is still ongoing. My grandfather's death certificate

Death Certificate of John Kruse.

gave his father's name as Honos Kruse. However, the place for the maiden name of his mother was blank. The informant was listed as his son Kenneth Kruse of Jamaica, New York, my uncle who was one year younger than I. My grandmother's death certificate was more than forty years older and did not call for the name of the informant. Her father's name was Matthias Wild. In the space that called for the maiden name of the mother, the words *Not Known* had been written. At this point, I had the names of six out of eight of my great-grandparents. My five-generation genealogical chart was really under way. In addition, a visit to my "uncle" Kenneth

Death Certificate of Catherine Kruse.

Birth Certificate of William Margolin.

seemed to be in order. Who else could give me better first
hand information about my grandfather and his family?

Meanwhile, I sent for a copy of the death certificate of my
father, who had died in California in 1966. By presenting a
copy of this document, I was able to obtain a copy of his birth
certificate. This document is usually the most difficult to obtain. In most cases, the birth certificate is only available to the
person named on it, his next of kin, and his immediate family. In any case, the only information on it that I didn't already
have was that when he was born in 1910, the Margolin family was living at 287 Henry Street in what was geographically
described as the Lower East Side of Manhattan.

Vital Records

Up to this point we have only dealt with four types of documents: the city directory, usually referred to as a C/D, the marriage license and death certificate, commonly known as the M/L and D/C respectively, and the birth certificate, which is shortened to B/C. The B/C, D/C, and M/L fall into the category of what are called "Vital Records." To the best of my knowledge, without exception, all of these records can only be obtained from some form of government agency. There are sometimes restrictions on their release. Each state and local government has its own rules. (The good news is that there are books on the library shelf that not only explain what these restrictions are, but provide blank forms that you can copy to obtain these documents.) The availability of vital records changes from state to state and from county to county. The key factor is usually how much time has passed since the birth or death occurred. It is now possible to obtain New York City birth records for anyone born before 1911 without any restrictions. There are usually several volumes available on most library shelves that tell which records are currently available throughout most of the United States. One of them is entitled the *Vital Records Handbook (see Appendix)*.

The city directory, or C/D, is one of the most important research tools. Even though it is not technically a vital record, the type of data it contains works well in conjunction with the other three. The information contained in these four sources, if properly used, can open up dozens of other areas for your research. How well you make use of them will usually make the difference between finding other leads or finding yourself at a standstill in your research. Bear in mind that with minimal use, I have already been able to identify six of my eight great-grandparents.

City directories were the forerunners of the telephone book. They have existed in America for more than 150 years and are still published annually in many American cities. The most famous is the directory published by R. L. Polk & Company. The 1933–1934 city directory for the Manhattan and Bronx boroughs of New York City was the last one published for that area. The size alone indicated that it was becoming unmanageable. When put on microfilm, it took up three rolls of film. I can only guess that they stopped publishing it because it became impossible to edit and reprint the data before it became obsolete.

The city directory is without doubt one of the best genealogical sources available. The only ones I have had the need to work with were pre-1935. Basically, they list the rich as well as the poor, and the black (referred to as colored) and the white. They also list the scavenger and the washerwoman, as well as the banker and the lawyer. They may also list the names of the policeman's wife and the doctor's children if they are over eighteen. Also included is the occupation and the address of the person at the time the directory was published. By going through these directories for a period of years, it is sometimes possible to determine when people arrived in the city as well as when they changed their residence. It is also possible to tell when young men married and left home to set up their own families. It also isn't too difficult to determine when people passed away or moved out of the city.

The marriage license is also a great source of information. It not only gives you information about the individuals getting married, but it also gives you the names of both of their parents. As with many vital records, the content of information contained changes from year to year as well as place to place. However, (in some states and counties) it contains at least the following basic information:

Name and Age of Groom
Name and Age of Bride
Home Address of Groom
Home Address of Bride
Name of Father of Groom
Maiden Name of Mother of Groom
Name of Father of Bride
Maiden Name of Mother of Bride
Where the Ceremony Took Place
Who Performed the Ceremony

Be extremely careful when ordering copies of marriage documents. Unless you specifically ask for a copy of the original license, you will usually receive a transcript. This does not always contain all the information contained in the original. A good example of this will be fully explained later on. Also remember that although the information in a marriage license was supplied by the individuals themselves, the information they had was given to them by their parents. For various reasons, the parents may have been mistaken about such things as the correct spelling of their own surname. This is also true about the correct spelling of the maiden names of the mothers of both the bride and the groom, which appears on virtually all marriage records. In addition, at the beginning of this century, there was no uniform spelling of common surnames. Nor was there much inquiry by public officials as to how a person spelled either his surname or given name. The official recording the data simply spelled it the way it sounded to him. This later accounted for many wasted hours hunting for a record under the name of Louis Smith, when it could have easily been found under Lewis Smyth.

The death certificate is also a great source of information. However, as with most vital records, the information con-

tained in it changes from year to year as the form is changed
to meet the needs of the government agency at that time.
Basically, most death certificates contained the following:

Name of Deceased
Home Address
Where Death Occurred
Cause of Death
Marital Status and Length
Occupation
Age
Date of Birth
Birthplace
Name of Father
Maiden Name of Mother
Name of Informant

In addition, death certificates in the early part of this century usually asked for the length of time the person had
lived in the United States, and the birthplace of each parent.
As you can see, the information is quite extensive and can
be used to open numerous other doors. For example, by
knowing how long the individual was married it is possible
to check the marriage license index and obtain a copy of
that document. The date of death and age at the time of
death can also lead you to a copy of the individual's birth
certificate. If the individual immigrated to the United States
in the early part of this century, it is also possible to locate
passenger arrival records by knowing the approximate year
the person arrived. There are numerous other helpful research possibilities.

One important fact about the information contained in a
death certificate is that it is not supplied by the person who
had passed away. It is usually supplied by a grieving hus-

band or wife, who may not be the best source for totally accurate information at that particular moment. Sometimes the information is supplied by a well-meaning relative such as a sister or brother, who only guesses at the accuracy of the facts. I can only add that sorting out fact from fiction is your job. As a matter of fact, that's what a good part of your job is all about.

Like the death certificate, the birth certificate contains information that is not supplied by the individual named in the document. However, little of the data relates directly to that person anyway. It does provide a great deal of useful information about a person's parents. Almost all birth certificates contain good basic information such as:

Name of Child
Date of Birth
Place of Birth
Name of Father
Age of Father
Occupation of Father
Address of Father
Birthplace of Father
Name of Mother
Age of Mother
Address of Mother
Maiden Name of Mother
Birthplace of Mother
Number of Previous Children
Number of Children Now Living
Name and Address of Person Making Report

If you have little knowledge about your family background, this information can be invaluable. It will tell you when your parents were born. If they were born in a foreign country, then your later search will probably involve passenger lists or naturalization papers. The occupation of the father can be very important. Even the number of previous children alerts you to the fact that other birth certificates exist. If not all are still living, then it can lead to a death certificate. All of this will be discussed in much more detail in a later chapter.

Research Etiquette

At this point, it might be a good idea to discuss a few things relating to genealogical research that many writers hesitate to cover in any detail for fear of offending some of their readers. Because I believe that it is germane to the degree of success you achieve in your research, I am certain that a small amount of in-depth coverage of these subjects is not only necessary, but mandatory. These items have been discussed at length with both librarians and researchers. For the most part, they agree in principle with what I am about to say.

The first comment deals with whatever claims you choose to make in your personal genealogical chart. It can be stated quite unequivocally that unless you can document each person you claim in your genealogical chart, you don't have a bona fide genealogy. If you start your genealogy with your grandfather and have no documentation linking you to him, then your genealogy is not valid. In genealogy, all claims must be documented before being validated. Even if no legal purpose is involved, no one seriously involved in genealogical research recognizes any claim when it is not documented. It is usually looked upon as little more than an ego trip. Perhaps the validity of this type of claim can best be illustrated with an example.

An incident occurred some time ago that was a classic example of egomania, absurdity, and stupidity combined. On a lesser scale, it is also indicative of how newcomers appear when they first become involved in genealogical research. The event occurred on a day when I was preparing to do some federal census research at the downtown Orlando Public Library. As I was signing the guest register, I stood next to a rather large, Tom Selleck look-alike, who was dressed in a custom-tailored jumpsuit with various colorful sports car auto patches on each arm. This was complemented by custom-made sneakers and a perfectly matched ascot. He was well spoken and obviously well educated. Because I had to wait my turn behind him, I couldn't help overhearing the conversation.

The young man was patiently and politely explaining that one of his close relatives had assured him that he was directly related to King Arthur. He wanted the librarian to search the records and authenticate that fact this afternoon, as he had a dinner engagement that evening and needed to present the proof to several members of his family. He was nice enough to add that he was prepared to spend the entire afternoon, if necessary, helping the librarian locate all the necessary documentation.

If the young man had not been so totally sincere, the absurdity and naiveté of this request would have been laughable. This same type of naiveté, on a smaller scale, is displayed almost daily by some who are already involved in genealogical research. In most cases, it is usually the first sign of a novice, and early on is usually overlooked by most librarians and research professionals. However, it is a totally annoying trait, which if not corrected will ultimately hinder progress. After a while these same librarians and other research professionals, who provide help and guidance, will stop going out of their way to aid and assist you. As it has been said, "A word to the wise should be sufficient."

A series of shops has opened in the Orlando area where I live. They claim to have genealogies on over 100,000 surnames. For a price, they will supply you with a mug, a coaster, or even a complete coat of arms, authenticated by their own researcher who doesn't appear to have any name except "Historian" along with the company name. While escorting several visitors through one of these shops, I overheard one of the clerks assuring a prospective customer that his family name could be authenticated and traced back to the eleventh century. Most serious genealogists know that common people didn't have surnames until a much later date. However, the clerk spoke with an air of authority that had the customer hypnotized. Two minutes later the same clerk was busy telling an attractive young lady that he was a part-time college student, whose only knowledge of genealogy was the information flashed before him on his computer screen. Another absurd situation, but this time gullible people were being taken in. If you seriously think that there is any quick and easy way to document your family heritage, then perhaps one of these shops is the place for you.

The second thing I want to mention falls under the general category of research facility etiquette and conduct, and also what I call, "doing your own homework." Etiquette and conduct are two things seldom mentioned in most books. When I first became involved in genealogical research, I quickly became aware that I was one of the youngest people in the room when I was visiting various research facilities. I was forty-six at the time. Recently, I have read several reports that stated that genealogy is the third largest hobby in America, and rapidly gaining ground on stamp and coin collecting.

Genealogy has attracted thousands of newcomers. The people who are now engaged in genealogical research come from every age group. The ethnic and social make up includes people from the entire spectrum of humanity. The current popularity of genealogy has also produced some problems. For example, the Orlando Public Library has several dozen microfilm readers. On a busy day, all are in use and there is a waiting line. In spite of this, there are people who totally ignore the posted time limits. There are others who leave their film on a machine and go to lunch, sometimes returning more than an hour later. There are polite signs asking users to limit their time when others are waiting, but these are ignored out of ignorance or indifference. I have seen researchers become verbally abusive because a librarian would not sit down at a microfilm reader and extract the information for them. There are dozens of variations of this type of immature behavior. The bottom line is that this type of offensive and abusive conduct is not acceptable under any circumstances.

In many cases, this type of conduct occurs out of ignorance rather than indifference or malice. If a person isn't aware of what the rules are, how can he or she be expected to follow them? In light of this fact, I have developed a code, which I apply to my own conduct when engaged in genealogical research. These are strictly my personal commandments of genealogy and I follow them daily. I have included a copy and I hope you might consider using them as a guideline. Everything in them is only a matter of common courtesy and common sense.

What I earlier referred to as "doing your own homework" is a far more complex matter. I have used the term homework for a good reason. It is a term we are all familiar with from our school days. The term *homework* in no way applied only to work that was done at home. It covered any assignment that was done outside of the classroom and outside of the supervision of a teacher. For our purposes, homework is meant to apply to any endeavor that involves

My Ten Commandments of Genealogical Research

by
Robert W. Marlin

1. Thou shalt master the art of patience, because without it thou art doomed to failure.
2. Thou shalt not engage in offensive conduct of any kind in public research areas. Unnecessary noise and chattering are especially annoying to others who are trying to concentrate.
3. Thou shalt be courteous and fair to others. Thou shalt not monopolize, abuse, or misuse any equipment.
4. Thou shalt be polite, patient, and extremely courteous when dealing with public officials, librarians, and others who work in research facilities.
5. Thou shalt come prepared to do thine own homework and not expect others to do it for you. This includes being equipped with your own tools, which include pencil and paper.
6. Thou shalt not attempt to bribe or offer gratuities to anyone in order to facilitate quick delivery or priority service on requests for records or information.
7. Thou shalt not knowingly invent or imagine false ties with ancestors who are not really your own, just for the sake of creating illustrious ancestors. Thou shalt make every attempt to document each and every ancestor one descends from.
8. Thou shalt share information found with other family members who have shared with you and supplied information that enabled you to go farther with your research.
9. Thou shalt never use any information gained to knowingly embarrass, belittle, or humiliate any other human being.
10. When in doubt, follow the Golden Rule.

learning how to do things for yourself. This can include anything from learning how to use a microfilm reader to writing a genealogical inquiry letter. It is not my intent to belabor the point. However, unless you know what is involved in the word *homework*, how can you be expected to do it? *The single most important thing in genealogical research is how well you learn to do your own homework.* As a Parris Island drill instructor is fond of saying when trying to emphasize a point, "This you can believe!"

Success or failure will depend on how well you do your homework. The English statesman, novelist, and prime minister, Benjamin Disraeli, once stated that "the secret of success is constancy of purpose." He was once misquoted as having said, "The secret of success is attention to detail." I personally like the latter definition. Either way, no statement could contain more truth when applied to genealogical research. How much success or failure you have will be totally related to how much attention is paid to detail and how constant you are in pursuit of your purpose. Only you can give your genealogy the attention to detail that it deserves. Don't ever think for a minute that anyone else cares as much about your genealogy as you do. Even your close relatives who may be interested in what you learn, would never give it the same amount of time and patience that you do. Once again, make no mistake about it, how much you will eventually get out of your research is directly related to how much effort you put into your work, and the work habits you develop will make the difference between success and failure.

There are now dozens of books about genealogy on the shelves of most libraries. Many are filled with endless information telling you where to write to obtain almost any kind of record. Inasmuch as the cost of public records and their location change constantly, many of these books are out of date almost by the time they are published. There are also many good books on the shelves of your local library, which deal in depth with many of the everyday things you must know in order to succeed. I strongly suggest that you spend some time reading a few of these books before ever starting out on your first search.

This book does not spend an inordinate amount of time explaining simple things, which in reality you can only learn by doing. This book was not written for dilettantes. It was written for the serious beginner or for the advanced beginner who has reached an impasse and needs help to shape or sharpen his or her techniques. This book is not designed to teach you how to operate a microfilm or microfiche machine. Nor will it teach you how to operate a copy machine. Only you teach yourself to do that.

Teach yourself how to break down a surname into a Soundex code before ever looking at a census sheet. Learn what the United States Census is all about and what it contains before ever starting a census search. Learn what immigration and passenger lists are available for which ports. It is not necessary to memorize all of this information. Just provide yourself with a general overview of what is available. Most of this general information can be learned in less than a couple of hours. You don't have to study every detail, only enough to make you able to operate on your own.

Most library equipment, such as microfiche and microfilm readers, is designed for consumer use and has a diagram and complete instructions on how to insert the film and operate the machine. All that is necessary is for you to read and follow the instructions. Modern-day copy machines are so easy to operate that no discussion is necessary. Librarians are more than happy to show newcomers how to use the various machines. After being shown, it is your job to develop skill in using this equipment. It is your job to search for and find the information you are looking for.

The various professionals and volunteers you encounter are only there to point the way. They are happy to give you an overview of what is available, but the hours you spend on microfiche and microfilm machines are the price you are going to pay in order to fulfill whatever goal you set for yourself. If you are properly doing your homework, then most of your questions to the librarians should involve seeking directions as to where the various sources are located within the library.

It is a total waste of everyone's time for you to spend ten minutes explaining everything you know about the Smith or Jones family. Try to realize that at least several hundred times a day librarians are hearing about different family names and couldn't possibly know, or even have the time to get overly involved in, your personal genealogy. Besides, it is not their job.

Their job is to point out where the census film is kept, not give you an education in what the federal census is all about. Their job is to show you where the material on French genealogy is located, not to give you an on-the-spot education on the subject. They can show you where the proper forms for ordering films and other materials are located, but they are not there to show you step-by-step how to fill out a form. You are expected to do that for yourself.

There is no one more apparent and foolish than the professional "brain picker," who is too lazy to do his or her homework and tries to take shortcuts and learn everything by picking the brains of others. Anyone can see through this type of leech who ends up with more misinformation than fact and never seems to get anywhere.

The rules regarding homework apply to all, including senior citizens like myself, who are not entitled to special treatment and coddling because of their age. The bottom line is that ultimately we must all learn to think and do for ourselves. That's also what success in genealogy is all about. And that is all I have to say in the way of admonitions.

It would not be in the reader's best interest to forget to mention a special group of people who contribute more to genealogical success than can truly be measured or appreciated. Without their help, modern genealogical research would slow down, if not come to a complete standstill. I am referring to the volunteers who run the libraries operated by the Church of Jesus Christ of Latter Day Saints, better known as the Mormon Church. They maintain Family History Center branches all over the country, allowing everyone to have access to records that would not be available any other way.

These branches are completely staffed by volunteers, whom I've found to be a most sincere, helpful, kind, courteous, and generally wonderful group of people. They are all involved in their own genealogy, which is part of being a Mormon. Many of these people work and raise families and still find time to help people outside of their church. I cannot praise them enough. However, the rules regarding doing your own homework apply here as well.

To give you a general overview of what is available from this source, consider this: Because of them I have had access to birth, death, and marriage records for New York City, even though I live in Florida. In addition, I've accessed everything from city directories for New York City to the Hamburg, Germany, passenger lists. On top of this I can access the Social Security Death Index via computer. On four CD-ROM disks that I can hold in the palm of my hand, it is possible for me to search through more than forty million names. The amount of material is almost limitless.

The main purpose of this book is to encourage you to think creatively. This book is also designed to teach you to take the information you find and use it to uncover more information. Use what you find to the best advantage and obtain the most available long-range mileage from it. This is what I call "creative analysis." When two people start out with identical information, one of the individuals is able to obtain four times as much information as his counterpart through creative analysis.

Some of my methodology may give you a headache. Don't fret. That's what it is designed to do. Some years ago a man named Einstein changed the world with a five symbol mathematical formula known as:

$$E = MC^2$$

My own mathematical formula for genealogical success is slightly more complex:

$$E + E1 + EE + SS = BRA$$
or

Effort + Enthusiasm + Extra Effort + Sheer Determination
=
Better Results Assured

By the way, there is absolutely no reason why you can't start your own genealogical chart right now. There is a blank chart on the next page. Make several photocopies. Blow one up for hanging on a wall. Start with yourself. Add both of your parents. If they are deceased, start now by obtaining documentation such as birth and death certificates. Order the death certificate first. The reason is simple. Many city and state governments will only issue a birth certificate to the person on the certificate. A copy of the death certificate and proof of your relationship will usually circumvent any problems in obtaining the birth certificate. By the time you receive the information, you should be finished with this book and ready to go out on your own.

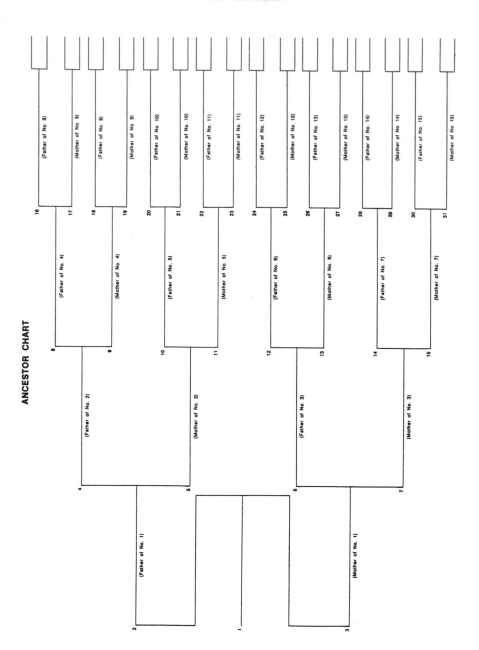

Ancestor chart—blank.

CHAPTER 3

Family Research Resumes

Shortly after the visit to my paternal grandparents' grave-stone at Montefiore Cemetery, I wrote a letter to Monte-fiore requesting whether or not the burial society known as the United Friends and Relatives still existed. They wrote back advising me that the society still existed and referred me to its recording secretary, a Mr. Jacob Levinson of Brooklyn. The letter included his address. Naturally, I got off a letter right away asking for any information he might have regarding my grandparents. He answered my letter almost immediately, letting me know that he personally knew my grandmother. A copy is shown on pages 54 and 55.

The letter was full of additional leads such as:

1. Another son named Teddy existed who must have been born in 1921, as he turned twenty-one in 1942.
2. Two additional addresses where my grandmother had lived.
3. My grandmother had a sister named Bella Sachar.
4. Willie Sachar certainly must be the son of Bella Sachar.

Dear Mr Robert W. Marlin

I've been very anxious to help you.
If you want to Know your family
that is root or tree. Or what par
of emigrate. The U.F & R. Org. of only re
Platives. I still have all minutes
from 1943 which I look over. We
used to meet every month. I've
been recording the minutes, mailin
Your grandmother Hilda was a sister
to Bella Sacher, society does not
Keep records place of birth r when
they came to this country. I looked
through the minutes of 11/43. Hilda
Frank claimed that a credit of 4.00
was due her for the year 1942 when
her son Teddy reached the age
of 21 and has been given credit
Willie & Ann Sacher 7 Lexington Ave.
N.Y.C 3 /1010 - You'll probably get some
information from them.

Hilda Frank lived in 2941 Brighton 5th St
Bklyn, 3034 Brighton 1st St. then 1008 Jefferson
Miami Beach, Florida.

                 Over -

Letter from Jacob Levinson. (Part-1)

your grandmother may she
rest in peace has been a very
friendly person. Came to all
the meetings.
When she lived in Brighton Beach.
came to see us very often.
The U. F. R. Org will appriciate
that you are willing to keep your
grandparents graves look good.
I wrote granddaughter in Buffalo
that her grandfathers graves is full
of weeds.
If I get any more information
I'll be t glad to write
Sorry I kept you waiting
that I can possibly help you.
You well deserve it.

                    Most Sincerely,
                    Jacob Levinson

Letter from Jacob Levinson. (Part-2)

5. My grandmother must have remarried as the letter refers
to her as Hilda Frank.

What amazed me was that this burial society still existed
and had records going back to the 1940s. Later research
shows that most Jewish records are more readily available
and much more thorough than many other forms of record
keeping. Mr. Levinson spoke so well of my grandmother that
I found myself forming a mental image of what she must
have been like. As time went on, this same type of mental
projection was used to create an image of each of the people I was researching. It was a delightful little game that
sometimes made the mundane part of research more exciting.

Several days later, I sent a letter to Willie Sachar explaining what I was trying to do. Within several days, I received
a phone call from Anne Sachar, inviting me over on a Sunday afternoon. To say that I was uncomfortable when I first
arrived would be an understatement, but they were quite
friendly and made me feel at home. Willie was indeed the
son of Bella Korris and Meyer Sachar. Because Hilda and
Bella were as close as sisters, he had practically grown up
with my father, William, and Uncle Paul. Willie had heard
that Paul had died in California several years earlier. He then
related numerous childhood adventures and in the course of
doing so mentioned his grandfather (my great-grandfather)
Hyman, who had died about 1924. Bella and Hilda also had
two brothers named Meyer and Abe. Meyer had lived in Buffalo, N.Y., and Abe had lived in Brooklyn. All four were now
deceased. Willie also remembered my grandfather Meyer.
He recalled that Meyer had invented many things and had
patented a number of them. He was certain that Meyer had
developed the modern-day wax crayon, but sold the rights
for a pittance before being able to patent the formula. He

also mentioned that he thought that my grandfather may have been previously married and that there might have been children from that marriage. All in all, it was a wonderful visit and we decided to get together again in the near future.

The following day, I received the death certificate for my grandmother Hilda. She had died in a nursing home in 1962. There was little additional information, except that my uncle Paul had been the informant. It gave his home address in Hollis, Queens, New York. A quick check revealed that he had long since moved. Several days later, I made a quick check of the New York City death index for 1924 and found that Willie Sachar had been exactly right regarding the year his grandfather (my great-grandfather) Hyman Korris had died. The next day I sent for a copy of his death certificate.

In the meantime, I called my uncle Ken and told him briefly about my Kruse family research. He seemed to be interested and invited me out to his home in Mineola, Long Island, to talk about what he knew about the family. I hadn't seen him since we were kids and I was surprised that he looked so much older than I. Ken came across in a most condescending manner, which clouded the interview and caused me to feel extremely uncomfortable. He insisted that everything he said had been related to him by his father and therefore was the gospel truth. He seemed to be letting me know that he was the Kruse family patriarch, in spite of the fact that my uncle John Jr. was his older brother. I overlooked as much of his superior attitude as I could, in the hope that enough truth would come to the surface to enable me to continue my research.

He started by looking at the death certificate I had received for his father and laughed. What looked like "Honos" to me was actually supposed to be Louis. As his narrative went, our great-grandfather's name was Louis Christian

Death Certificate of Hilda Margolin.

Kruse. He had married Lena Bernhard and they had sailed from Copenhagen, Denmark, to America sometime in the mid-1850s. Lena was supposedly related to Sarah Bernhard, although the relationship was unknown and undocumented. Louis C. Kruse died when John Sr. was a boy, but no one seemed to remember when Lena Bernhard Kruse had passed away. There were other bits of embellishment to his story, but I had already decided that other than the names of the people and possibly the date of Louis's death, most of the rest of the story was wrong. I listened politely as he continued to tell other little stories that were obvious fabrications.

For example, he tried to convince me that his father had been a devout Catholic when he was married to my grandmother. This was quite strange considering that the Kruse family had owned a twelve-grave-site family burial plot at Lutheran Cemetery in Queens. Ken couldn't explain how John Sr. had obtained the middle name of Patrick. I asked this question several times, but my inquiry was ignored. He insisted on telling several other inane family stories, which I listened to and promptly dismissed as absurd. This was one of the worst interviews I had ever experienced, but it was a learning experience.

Finding my grandfather in the birth index was simple now, as I already knew within a couple of years when his birth occurred. It turned out to be September 13, 1882. Assuming that Ken was right about Louis C. Kruse dying while John was still a boy, I was also about to pinpoint his death. The death index for 1891 shows the date to be September 8, 1893. Naturally, the first thing I did was to send for copies of the certificates for each event.

A trip to the patent division of the New York Public Library provided me with a stunning discovery. Starting with the year 1900, it was a simple matter to check the yearly indexes. In no time I had found not one, but three items that my paternal grandfather had patented between 1904 and 1907. One of them was a real mindblower. It was a patent for what my grandfather had named "Combination Furniture." It was a chair, which at night turned into a bed. Sound familiar? I found it hard to believe. All these years I had believed that the Castro Convertible Co. invented the convert-

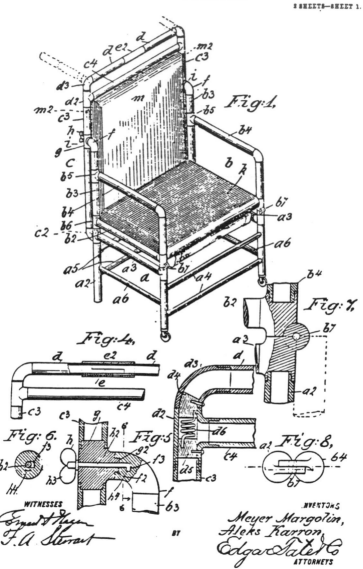

No. 855,520.

PATENTED JUNE 4, 1907.

M. MARGOLIN & A. KARRON.

COMBINATION FURNITURE.

APPLICATION FILED AUG. 4, 1906.

2 SHEETS—SHEET 1.

Diagram of Combination Furniture. (Part-1)

No. 855,520.

PATENTED JUNE 4, 1907.

M. MARGOLIN & A. KARRON.
COMBINATION FURNITURE.
APPLICATION FILED AUG. 4, 1906.

2 SHEETS—SHEET 2.

Fig. 2,

Fig. 3,

WITNESSES

INVENTORS
Meyer Margolin,
Aleks Karron,
BY
Edgar Tate & Co.
ATTORNEYS

Diagram of Combination Furniture. (Part-2)

ible bed. Now I had proof that my Jewish grandfather had actually invented it.

Several weeks later, I received the death certificate of Louis C. Kruse and the birth certificate of John Patrick Kruse. The death certificate showed that my maternal great-grand-father had accidentally drowned on September 8, 1893. The death certificate also stated that the incident had occurred at the "foot of Atlantic Avenue" in Brooklyn, New York. It also gave his age as fifty, his occupation as rigger, his place of birth as Denmark, and his home address as 160 North 3rd Street in the 14th Ward of the borough of Brooklyn. Wards are simply political subdivisions of an area for voting purposes and are still used today. This event was reported in the Brooklyn *Eagle* newspaper the next day. It simply stated that Lewis Krusa, age fifty-five, had fallen off a dock and drowned. Please note that the spelling of both the surname and given name, as well as the age, were in error. This is typical of what you can run into when doing family research. Later research showed that the term rigger meant ship's rigger or ship's carpenter. This was certainly plenty of information with which to begin a complete search.

My grandfather's birth certificate was a treasure trove of information. He was born on September 13, 1882. John was born at 366 1/2 Ewen Street, which as I said earlier, was less than a mile from where he died. As I suspected, his middle name was not Patrick. Only the initial "H" was given. This undoubtedly stood for Henry, which was later found to be the middle name of several other Kruse children. His father's name was Louis C. Kruse and his mother's name was Lena Bernhard. My uncle Ken had been right about that part. Lena was thirty-five years old and Louis was thirty-nine. His occupation was listed at this time as paver. An important piece of information was that he was the eighth child born to this woman. This meant that at least five of those children

Death Certificate of Lewis C. Kruse.

didn't live to see the year 1900. Two equally important pieces of information were that Louis had been born in Denmark, and that Lena had been born in Germany. This confirmed my suspicion that they didn't come to America together. More on them later.

Brooklyn Eagle
Report of Death Louis C. Kruse
6 September 1893

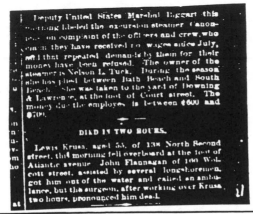

DIED IN TWO HOURS

Lewis Krusa, age 55, of 138 North Second
street, this morning fell overboard at the foot of
Atlantic Avenue. John Flannagan of 160 Wolcott street,
assisted by several longshoremen, got him out of the
water and called an ambulance, but the surgeon, after
working over Krusa for two hours, pronounced him dead.

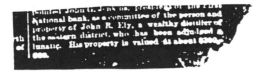

Death report of Louis C. Kruse from the Brooklyn Eagle *newspaper.*

Birth Certificate of John H. Kruse.

When the death certificate for Hyman Korris arrived, it contained the names of his parents. On the surface this may seem like just more information. It gave his father's name as William Korris and his mother's name as Roshi (Rose) Levy. These were the first of my great-great-grandparents that I had been able to find and document. It also gave Hyman's birth year as 1849, and recorded that he had been in the United States eighteen years. Naturally, it also listed the cemetery where the gravesite was located. By now, my hope is that you are able to see the significance and connections between all these seemingly unrelated dates and facts.

Anne Sachar called me the following week to invite me to the annual banquet of the United Friends and Relatives Society. It was held in a restaurant on Kings Highway in Brooklyn. Even the location was significant, in that a good many of the present members of the society, most of whom were direct descendants of the founders, had all been born and raised in Brooklyn. It turned out to be a great event for me because I met numerous people who had known my grandmother personally. All of them had nice things to say.

However, all of them independently referred to her as a "sweet, gentle lady." One woman, named Vivian Myerson, also knew my father. Her mother was the sister of Bella Sachar's husband, Meyer. She remembered seeing my father when he came home on leave from the Navy in the 1920s. Vivian was extremely interested in my research and even offered to see what she could find out from other relatives.

Vivian called me a week later and asked if I would like to visit her aunt, Jenny Cherson, who was a "multifamily matriarch" by virtue of her age. She was in her late eighties and lived in New Jersey with her son. Naturally, I jumped at the chance to meet someone who must have known both of my grandparents, as well as their children. Vivian made the necessary arrangements and we drove down the following week.

On the trip down, Vivian explained to me that at one time all Jewish families had an "Aunt Jenny." The name may have actually been Rosie, Sarah, Becky, or even Hilda. There was also a male counterpart named Uncle Irving, Hymie, or Ike. The common denominator was that each of them was the sole surviving family member of a generation of Jews who truly belonged to another generation. They were the last of the generation to be born in Europe or Russia, and then immigrated to America. They came as late as 1910 and yet survived late into the twentieth century. They were also the custodians and unofficial family record keepers of many family secrets, both good and bad.

When I met Aunt Jenny she was in her late eighties. No one was sure exactly when she was born. Modern Americans don't seem to realize that the celebration of a birthday is a comparatively modern custom. In the old country there were many reasons for Jews to conceal and lie about their age. Being drafted into the Russian Army for twenty-five years was just one of them. In any case, Aunt Jenny looked

Death Certificate of Hyman Korris.

and dressed like someone from another generation, if not
another world. Mentally, she was an astounding woman.
She had a memory that produced almost total recall of people and events that had taken place many decades before. I
had been cautioned before the meeting that note-taking
made her nervous. Therefore, I would have to depend upon

my own memory to record any information I wanted to save until after the meeting was over.

Vivian and I listened for more than two hours while she talked almost nonstop. She remembered my grandfather and didn't try to hide her disdain. She referred to him as a Litvak, a term Vivian had to explain. A Litvak was someone who was from the section of Russia known as Belorussia, which included the Oblast (province) of Minsk. At one time the area was part of Lithuania, hence the name Litvak. Most of my grandmother's family came from an area about halfway between the cities of Kiev and Odessa, in the Ukraine. The Ukrainian Jews looked down their noses at the Litvaks the same way as most German Jews look down their noses at Russian Jews. She talked about my grandmother with genuine fondness, as well as her sisters. Abruptly, Aunt Jenny decided that it was time for her nap, indicating that the interview was over.

On the way back, we stopped for coffee and I took the time to jot down everything I could remember that might be relevant to my research. When I finished there were only four items, but it would take me a number of years to verify all that they represented. They were:

1. My grandmother Hilda had made a trip back to Russia after marrying my grandfather Meyer in 1904. It was for the purpose of making arrangements for her father and brothers to come to America.
2. Her oldest son, my uncle Sam, had been born while she was in Russia.
3. My grandmother's sister Rose had married Ike Siegel in 1901. He was in the hardware business.
4. Ike had a brother named Meyer who became a lawyer.

At the time of my meeting with Aunt Jenny, I was new to the art of the oral interview and felt that although the meeting was interesting, the amount of information gained was minimal. I even wondered at the time just how accurate I would find it to be. After all, she was an old lady and many of the events she related had occurred almost seventy-five years ago.

Within three months I had located and fully documented the first two items listed above. By checking through passenger list indexes, I was able to find out that my grandmother and Uncle Sam returned to the United States on May 5, 1906, on board the S.S. *Zeeland*. A copy of the passenger manifest records her name as Margulis, and the relative she would be rejoining was her husband, M. Margulis, residing at 287 Henry Street. This is the same address recorded on my father's birth certificate as described earlier. This is a typical example of how the pieces of the puzzle slowly come together. Also, as I stated earlier, don't allow yourself to get hung up over the correct spelling of anything. Whether it's the first name, last name, or place, you will always find different spellings.

Further research in the index located the arrival of Hilda's father, Hyman Korris. He and his sons arrived in New York on May 8, 1906, aboard the S.S. *Noordland*. This information was slightly more difficult to find because of the way his name was spelled on the passenger manifest. He was listed as "Chaim Kuraris," age fifty-three. (Note that this does not match the age shown on his death certificate.) He arrived accompanied by his three sons, Abe, Wely, and Meir. (Once again, note the spellings of the boys' names.) Wely simply is a badly spelled version of the Hebrew name Velvel. The English version of the name is William. Obviously, both this boy and my father, William, had been named after Hyman's father. Their final destination was with his daughter Bella Kuraris, c/o P. Boudin, who lived at 617 Metropolitan Avenue in Brooklyn. Bella was his daughter as well as my

Passenger Arrival List, S.S. Zeeland, listing Hilda and Sam Margolin.

grandmother's sister. P. Boudin was Bella and Hilda's Uncle Peter who you will learn more about later.

These two discoveries now gave me six people to research more thoroughly. Naturally, the research done on each of these six individuals continued to produce new information and new leads. Additional leads seemed to appear *ad infinitum*. After five years, the original six people had grown to twenty and in ten years the number was more than fifty. As a direct result of these two new bits of information that Aunt Jenny supplied, I have been able to locate aunts, uncles, and cousins, in Seattle, Los Angeles, Florida, New Jersey, and Virginia.

It took a long time to solve the riddle of the Siegel family. The first thing I looked for was a record of the marriage between Ike Siegel and Rose Korris. There were a number of men named Isaac Siegel who had married in 1901. I paid a professional researcher to check all of them out. None matched my information. It was low-priority research so I spot-checked death certificates and censuses while looking for other things. I never located information on Ike or Rose.

During one of my conversations with Willie, he told me that his father's family name had originally been Siegel. For some unknown reason the name had been changed to Sachar. I later found out something that had not been apparent to me and that no one had mentioned. Aunt Jenny's maiden name was Siegel and she was Willie's father's sister. They also had a brother named Isadore. Was this the Ike I was looking for? Over a long period of time I researched the Sachar and Siegel families, but never found any information that linked any of them to Ike Siegel and Rose Korris. I finally became convinced that somehow Aunt Jenny was confused about items three and four that she had related to me.

My files contain several well-packed folders filled with information I have collected, but have not been able to relate

Passenger Arrival List, S.S. Noordland, listing Chaim, Abraham, Veley and Meir Kuraris.

to my research. I go through these files at least four or five times a year. One year while browsing, I came across a naturalization card for Isaac W. Siegel who had been naturalized in 1898. Also in my possession were the papers of his father, David Siegel. These papers had been in my possession for more than ten years and I had never been able to connect them to my own family. This time, however, the thing that caught my eye was not the name of the person naturalized, but the name of the witness to the event. It was Louis P. B. Boudin, who was a first cousin to my grandmother and the son of Peter Boudin. I had finally made a family connection. The next step was to document the connection.

This time I was determined to do the research myself. I went to the Family History Center at the Latter Day Saints Church and found that they had on hand the marriage license index for New York City for the year 1901. I only came up with two men named Isaac Siegel who had gotten married in 1901. Only one of them used the middle initial "W." I sent for a copy of that certificate immediately. At the same time, I resolved that never again would I stop searching for information simply because someone else had searched and not found it. Either I would search for it myself, or if that was not possible, have the source checked at least three different times by different researchers.

When the license arrived, the amount of information it contained was outstanding. Ike and Rose were married on August 30, 1901. Ike was Isaac William Segal, the son of David Siegal and Katie Boudin. (Once again, note the spelling.) Rosie was the daughter of Hyman Koris and Pessie Boudiansky. Ike was twenty-five and Rose was nineteen. My grandfather Meyer Margolin was one of the witnesses. The other witness was Meyer Boudiansky, who was also known as Rabbi Meyer Budinoff. You will read more about him later. Also, the mother of the bride and the mother of the groom were sisters. So, the bride and groom were first cousins. (Once again, forget how the names are spelled.) Both of the mothers were, in turn, the sister of Peter Boudin.

The marriage license also lists the home address of the Segal family as 15 Rutgers Place on the Lower East Side of Manhattan. Using that address, I was able to locate the entire family in the federal census of 1900. At that time the family name was listed as Siegelman. It consisted of David, Gitel (Katie), Bernard, Isaac, and another son named Meyer who was attending school. I was later able to verify that this was the Meyer Siegel who became a lawyer and had a brother named Ike. The explosion process started all over again. Each discovery produced more leads, which continued to appear faster than I could follow them up.

Sometime later, while searching through the Social Security death index, I discovered that Aunt Jenny Cherson had passed away in 1984. I tried to obtain a copy of her death certificate, but was informed that the state of New Jersey had temporarily discontinued mail requests for genealogical information. In retrospect, the important thing is that all the information related by Aunt Jenny proved to be totally correct in every detail. Only my own ignorance and complacency prevented me from verifying this information sooner. The only thing I can say at this point is, "Aunt Jenny, I thank you for everything."

Marriage License of Isaac W. Segal and Rosie Korras. (Part-1)

We, the Groom and Bride named in this Certificate, hereby certify, that the information given therein is correct, to the best of our knowledge and belief.

Marriage License of Isaac W. Segal and Rosie Korras. (Part-2)

CHAPTER 4

My Mother's Story Continues

When I arrived for the second oral interview with my mother, I found her attitude totally different from the first. She almost couldn't wait to get started. She had let me know in advance exactly what she wanted to discuss. Mother wanted to discuss what she knew about her mother's side of her family. This was obviously a subject that brought her some pleasant memories, because her entire attitude was the opposite of what it had been when we were discussing the Kruse family.

Her mother, Catherine Wild Kruse, had died when she was only nine years old. She still had vivid memories of her mother, in spite of the short time they had spent together. These fond memories extended to her grandparents, Matthias and Maria Wild. Maria had died when my mom was only five, but she vividly remembered being cared for and pampered by her. After the death of her mother, Matthias paid special attention to these grandchildren, even though he had many others through his other sons and daughters. Mother and her sisters responded years later by visiting Matthias regularly. They visited him at least twice a month.

It was a long trolley ride and walk, or they would have visited weekly. By then he was a resident at the Kings County Home for the Aged in Brooklyn, where he died in 1926.

During these visits to the nursing home my mother remembered hearing many family anecdotes, but little of genealogical importance. Matthias spoke of his boyhood somewhere in the Alsace-Lorraine region of France and professed some skill in the art of wine-making. Boston of the 1880s had little need for skilled wine-makers, but he was able to obtain work as a brewer for short periods of time. However, most of the time he had to work as a laborer in order to support his growing family. His reason for coming to America was simple. He was what we now call a draft-dodger. Even he saw himself in that role. Because of him, I made some effort to learn a little more of the history of what is now known as the Franco-Prussian War. Briefly, in 1866 what had been a large number of disorganized small German states all joined the kingdom of Prussia. This was known as the Zollverein. In 1867 and 1868 the Zollverein annexed Alsace and Lorraine as well as other territories near their borders. They were then known as the New Zollverein. After the Franco-Prussian War, which started in 1870, Alsace and Lorraine became part of the German Confederation.

My mother described how amused her grandfather was when he told the story. He laughed when he described running away to America to avoid being conscripted into the Prussian Army. He made it sound like they were right behind him when he "ran like hell to get away." Inasmuch as he always thought of himself as a Frenchman, the thought of serving on the Prussian side of the conflict must have been an intolerable concept.

Matthias and Maria had parented seven children of their own. There was John, Joseph, Frank, George, my grandmother Katherine, Louisa, and Mary. All of the children were born in Boston. For unknown reasons the family had moved to Brooklyn after the Great Blizzard of 1888. Katherine was born in 1882, which meant that the other six were born in years on either side of that date. My mother thought that the boys may have come along first, but she was not sure.

The Census and Soundex

By this time, I had already started to learn all I could about the United States Federal Census. The story is basically simple. There has been a federal census taken in the United States every ten years since 1790. At the time that I started to do census research, the latest one open to the public was for the year 1900. (Since then, both the 1910 and 1920 federal censuses have been opened to the public. Both of these will be discussed at greater length in a later chapter.) The only exception was the federal census of 1890. Almost all of it was destroyed by a fire. Each of these early censuses contained family information that varied greatly in its value to genealogists. The earlier ones contained the least amount, while the later ones progressively provided better and more detailed information. All the federal censuses from 1790 through 1860 have been indexed and these indexes are available in book form in most libraries with genealogical facilities.

At the time the 1900 census was released, there was no doubt that it was by far the most comprehensive census ever taken. It was the first one to include not only the present age at the time of the census, but also the year and month of birth. It included the number of years the head of household was married as well as the relationship between each person and the head of the household.

Also included was the year of immigration to the United States and the number of years in the United States. This figure can sometimes be helpful when you are searching passenger lists. Suppose you are searching the 1900 census and find that someone you are searching for immigrated in 1870. However, the schedule shows the person to be living in America for only twenty-nine years. This census was started on June 1, 1900. Therefore, this would seem to indicate that the person immigrated after June 1st of the year in which they arrived, or the schedule would show them living in the U.S. for thirty years.

The census included the occupations of all family members, the language they spoke, and the place of their birth. It also included an entry that sometimes makes it easier to account for all the members of a family. This was in the form of two short questions. "How many children has the wife had?" and "How many are still living?" This census listed the complete street address where the family was living. The 1910 and 1920 censuses are also quite detailed, but in my opinion they are not as helpful as the 1900 census.

The 1880 census had a new feature that was totally unique. It was the first census to have what is known as a Soundex index. This is briefly explained on the next page. Every name can be broken down into a code, which contains a letter followed by three digits. There are pages in this book that explain the basics. What I have included should be more than enough to get you started. One additional important fact applies only to the 1880 Soundex. It includes only heads of households in which there was a child of ten years of age or younger. If the people you are looking for in the 1880 Soundex did not have a child ten or under in the household, you are wasting your time. One other point to remember: All censuses having Soundex consist of two sets of film. One contains the indexed Soundex cards and the other contains the actual census schedules.

Statement of a little-known fact about all of these census indexes is in order. All of them were put together in the mid-1930s at the height of what is now referred to as the "Great Depression." The purpose at the time was to create jobs for millions of out-of-work Americans. This work for the most part was performed by people who were in no way professional researchers, regular government employees, or even skilled clerks. They all were people who were simply doing what they had to do in order to survive. All in all, I think they did a fantastic job. Without these indexes, the job of the genealogist would be many times more difficult. However, in spite of the basic success of their endeavor, there are hundreds of errors and omissions. You, as a dedicated researcher, must learn to recognize and overcome these minor problems. In a later chapter I'll show you how to search most federal censuses without the use of Soundex.

If you are starting to do your own homework, you will quickly discover that instruction manuals exist that explain in a lot more detail how each of the censuses work and the differences between them. They are available through the National Archives and are listed in the Appendix. The detailed information in these manuals is not something that you should expect a librarian to explain in detail. Copies of these manuals are generally available at the reference desk of any library that has genealogical film. There are basically four manuals. The first one covers the censuses from 1790 to 1890. The other three cover the years 1900, 1910, and 1920 respectively. It is my strong recommendation that you purchase a copy of each of these. They only cost a couple of dollars each and will save you a lot of time.

Finding the Wild family in the 1900 census was easy. They were at that time living in the Greenpoint section of Brooklyn, less than a mile from where my mother lives to this day. You can see from the example on the next page that the information provided enabled me to go in any number of directions in order to gain more information. According to this document, Matthias and Maria must have been married shortly before immigrating to the United States. It also listed both of their places of birth as Germany. Obviously, this is an error.

Another little-known fact about the census is that census takers then were the same as census takers now. They were people earning extra money working at a temporary second job. The job of census taker was usually clearly outlined. One thing they were not authorized or required to do was verify any of the information obtained during a census interview with a family. Their job was to record what they were told. If the people being interviewed did not speak English, this created more problems. Either a neighbor had to act as an interpreter, or some guesswork was necessary. Because of this necessary guesswork, many discrepancies exist in public records. If the person being interviewed spoke with what may have sounded like a German accent, it is possible that the census taker simply recorded the birthplace as Germany. A person speaking German could easily have come from the border areas of such countries as France or Denmark. Many of those countries' borders changed many times. Learning some political geography will certainly be an asset when you start exploring any European ancestors.

After finding the Wild family in the 1900 census and analyzing the facts it contained, I decided that I wanted to know more about their life in Boston. With the information I now had it would be much easier to check birth records, city directories, and possibly Boston passenger arrival lists.

1900 U.S. Census—Matbias Wild and Family.

Boston is a lovely city filled with American history and it is an almost never ending source of history and genealogy. The Boston Public Library is one of the best in the country and their personnel are professional, courteous, and first rate. At that time, book copies of city directories were available right on the shelf. Because the census showed my grandmother being born in 1882, I started there and worked my way forward and then backward. As you can see, the results were extremely good. Out of the twenty years checked, I found city directory entries for ten of them. A quick check of city maps indicated that all of these street addresses were in the Roxbury section of Boston. All of this research was accomplished in less than two hours.

BOSTON CITY DIRECTORY

YEAR	LISTING	OCCUPATION	ADDRESS
1875	Wilde, M.	Finisher	15 Fellows Ct.
1879	Wild, Mack	Laborer	133 Hallock St.
1882	Wild, Mathias	Brewer	135 Hallock St.
1883	Wild, Mathias	Laborer	Heath Place
1884	Wild, Mathias	Laborer	28 Mindoro
1885	Wild, Mathias	Laborer	28 Mindoro
1886	Wild, Mathias	Laborer	28 Mindoro
1887	Wild, Mathias	Laborer	24 Russell
1888	Wild, Mathias	Laborer	24 Field
1889	Wild, Mathias	Laborer	24 Field

A quick trip to the Vital Records Bureau made me aware that getting birth certificates would take some time. The birth index was not available for public use at that time. I picked up all the necessary forms, but decided to wait until I got back from my trip and fill them out at my leisure.

My next stop was the Boston branch of the National Archives, which is located in Waltham, a suburb of Boston. They had copies of naturalizations that took place in the area. In less than an hour, I had located the naturalization papers of Matthias Wild. There was little doubt that he was the right one. It was a simple two-page document, but to me it truly represented a passport to the past. It clearly listed his occupation as brewer and his place of birth as Souls [sic], France. It also indicated that as an American citizen he renounced any allegiance to the Republic of France. His home address was listed as 28 Mindoro Street, which was consistent with the city directory information. The other two items listed were not consistent with other documents. For example, it listed his date of birth as February 5, 1845. It also stated that he immigrated to the United States on the tenth of May in the year 1862. But as far as I was concerned, obtaining this document alone made the entire trip worthwhile.

Within four weeks after my return from Boston, I received three letters in the mail. One was a thick envelope containing birth certificates for four of the Wild children. This included one for my grandmother Catherine. Each of the others contained a death certificate. One was for Matthias Wild, and the other was for his wife, Maria. The four birth certificates contained little that I didn't already know. The occupation of brewer appeared for Matthias in one of them. The birthplace as France also showed up on one out of the four.

The death certificates for Maria and Matthias were far more rewarding. Matthias gave his age as eighty-one, which made his birth year 1845. This was consistent with the information on his naturalization papers. Figures showing the number of years in the United States and the number of years living in New York City were totally inconsistent with

To the Honorable the Judges of the **Circuit Court of the United States,**
begun and holden at Boston, within and for the District of Massachusetts.

Respectfully represents _Mathias Wild_
of _Boston,_ _28 Hudson St_ in said District, occupation, _Bremer_
an Alien and a free white person; that he was born in _Souls_
France

on or about
the _fifty_ day of _February_ in the year of our Lord eighteen
hundred and _forty five_ and is now about _Thirty eight_ years of
age; that he arrived at _New York_ in the District of
in the United States of America, on or about the
Tenth day of _May_ in the year of our Lord eighteen
hundred and _Sixty two_ being then a minor under the age of eighteen years;
that it then was, and still is, his bona fide intention to reside in and become a citizen
of the United States of America, and to renounce all allegiance and fidelity to every
foreign Prince, State, Potentate, and Sovereignty whatsoever — more especially to
~~Victoria, Queen of the United Kingdom of Great Britain and Ireland,~~
whose subject he has heretofore been.
~~And the said petitioner further represents that he made a primary declaration~~
~~of his intention to become a citizen of the said United States, before the Honorable~~
Court,
on the   day of   A. D. 188
And the said petitioner further represents that he has ever since continued
to reside within the jurisdiction of the United States; that he has never borne
any hereditary title, or been of any of the orders of nobility; that he is ready to
renounce and abjure all allegiance and fidelity to every foreign Prince, Potentate,
State or Sovereignty whatsoever; and particularly to ~~Victoria, Queen of the~~
~~United Kingdom of Great Britain and Ireland,~~
Republic of France
whose subject he has heretofore been; that he is attached to the principles of the
Constitution of the United States of America, and well disposed towards the good
order and happiness of the same.
~~And the said petitioner further represents that he enlisted in the Armies of~~
~~the United States, and was honorably discharged therefrom.~~
Wherefore, your petitioner prays that he may be admitted to become a
citizen of the said United States of America, according to the forms of the Statutes
in such case made and provided.

Mathias Wild

188   . Sworn to by said Petitioner before the Court.
Attest:

_................................_ ....Clerk.

Naturalization Paper of Mathias Wild. (Part-1)

United States of America.

Massachusetts District, to wit, CITY OF BOSTON, *Oct. 18.* 188 *3*

We *Alexander C. Forbes, 14 Sewall Place Boston*

Bartholomew Zeller Boylston St. Jamaica Plain

and both citizens of said United States, severally depose and say, that we have known the foregoing petitioner for five years last past, during which time he has resided in said *Boston*

and that he has resided within the State of Massachusetts one year at least; and has conducted himself and behaved as a man of good moral character, attached to the principles of the Constitution of the United States, and well disposed towards the good order and happiness of the same.

Oct. 18. 1883. Sworn to by the above-named Witnesses, before the Court.

Attest:

_____, *Clerk.*

OATH TAKEN BY PETITIONER.

I, *Matthias Wild* do solemnly swear, that I do absolutely and entirely renounce and abjure all allegiance and fidelity to every Foreign Prince, Potentate, State or Sovereignty whatsoever, — particularly to **Victoria**, Queen of the United Kingdom of Great Britain and Ireland,

whose subject I have heretofore been; and that I will support the Constitution of the United States of America, — so help me God.

Mathias Wild

United States of America.

District of Massachusetts, to wit:

At a Circuit Court of the United States, begun and holden at said Boston, on the fifteenth day of *October* in the year of our Lord 188*3*, to wit, on the *18th* day of *October* A. D. 188*3*, the said *Wild* having produced the evidence required by law, took the aforesaid oath and was admitted to become a citizen of the United States of America; and the Court ordered that record thereof be made accordingly.

Attest:

_____ *Clerk.*

_____

Naturalization Paper of Mathias Wild. (Part-2)

Form R-54. 15M

𝕿𝖍𝖊 𝕮𝖔𝖒𝖒𝖔𝖓𝖜𝖊𝖆𝖑𝖙𝖍 𝖔𝖋 𝕸𝖆𝖘𝖘𝖆𝖈𝖍𝖚𝖘𝖊𝖙𝖙𝖘

STATE DEPARTMENT OF PUBLIC HEALTH

REGISTRY OF VITAL RECORDS AND STATISTICS

N⁰ 43721

COPY OF RECORD OF BIRTH

I, the undersigned, hereby certify that I am the Registrar of Vital Records and Statistics: that as such have custody of the records of birth required by law to be kept in my office; that among such records : one relating to the birth of

CATHARINE   WILD

and that the following is a true copy of so much of said record as relates to said birth, namely:—

Name   CATHARINE   WILD

Date of Birth   JANUARY 31, 1883

Place of Birth   BOSTON MASS.

Sex F   Color WHITE

FATHER		MOTHER	
Name	MATTHEW	Maiden Name	MARY
Residence	HEATH ST. PL. BOSTON	Residence	HEATH ST. PL. BOSTON
Birthplace	GERMANY	Birthplace	GERMANY
Occupation	LABORER	Occupation	

Date of Record   1883

And I do hereby certify that the foregoing is a true copy from said records.

WITNESS my hand and the GREAT SEAL OF THE COMMONWEALTH a Boston on this   13TH   day of JULY   19 79

HERBERT E. RISSER, JR.
Registrar of Vital Records and Statistic

Year	1883
Vol.	342
Page	196
No.	8798

Birth Certificate of Catherine Wild.

Death Certificate of Mathias Wild.

any other information found to date. It did list his occupation as brewer. Last, but certainly not least, it gave the name of his father and the maiden name of his mother. His father was Peter Wild and his mother was Catherine Wenoel. Now I had two more great-grandparents to add to my chart. I almost overlooked one item that meant little to me at the time. It was his home address, which was given as 338 39th Street, Brooklyn. I found out much later that this was the address

Death Certificate of Maria Wild.

of the Kings County Home for the Aged. It was then that I realized that the information on the certificate was taken from information that Matthias himself had supplied to the home and was probably extremely accurate. I'm certain that no one there dreamed up the names of his parents.

The death certificate for Maria was less informative. It gave her age as sixty-eight years, eleven months, and seventeen days. If this was accurate, she had been born on June

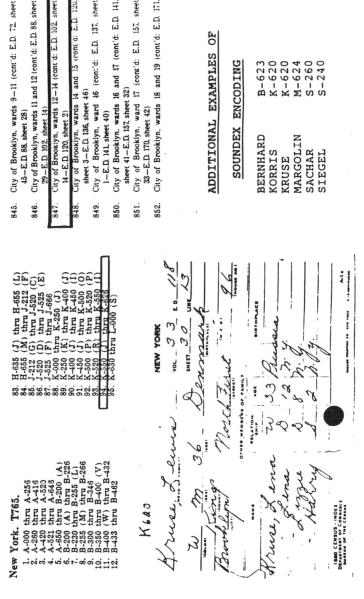

845. City of Brooklyn, wards 9—11 (cont'd: E.D. 72, sheet 45—E.D. 88, sheet 28)

846. City of Brooklyn, wards 11 and 12 (cont'd: E.D. 88, sheet 29—E.D. 102, sheet 14)

847. City of Brooklyn, wards 12—14 (cont'd: E.D. 102, sheet 14—E.D. 120, sheet 2)

848. City of Brooklyn, wards 14 and 15 (cont'd: E.D. 120, sheet 3—E.D. 136, sheet 46)

849. City of Brooklyn, ward 16 (cont'd: E.D. 137, sheet 1—E.D. 141, sheet 40)

850. City of Brooklyn, wards 16 and 17 (cont'd: E.D. 141, sheet 41—E.D. 157, sheet 32)

851. City of Brooklyn, ward 17 (cont'd: E.D. 157, sheet 33—E.D. 170, sheet 42)

852. City of Brooklyn, wards 18 and 19 (cont'd: E.D. 171.

ADDITIONAL EXAMPLES OF

SOUNDEX ENCODING

BERNHARD	B-623
KORRIS	K-620
KRUSE	K-620
MARGOLIN	M-624
SACHAR	S-260
SIEGEL	S-240

New York. T765.

1. A-000 thru A-256
2. A-260 thru A-416
3. A-420 thru A-520
4. A-521 thru A-645
5. A-650 thru B-200 (A)
6. B-200 (A) thru B-226
7. B-230 thru B-255 (L)
8. B-255 (M) thru B-266
9. B-300 thru B-346
10. B-350 thru B-400 (V)
11. B-400 (W) thru B-432
12. B-433 thru B-462

83. H-635 (J) thru H-655 (L)
84. H-655 (M) thru J-212 (F)
85. J-212 (G) thru J-520 (C)
86. J-520 (D) thru J-525 (E)
87. J-525 (F) thru J-666
88. K-000 thru K-250 (J)
89. K-250 (K) thru K-400 (J)
90. K-400 (J) thru K-450 (O)
91. K-450 (J) thru K-500 (O)
92. K-500 (P) thru K-520 (P)
93. K-520 (R) thru K-550 (I)
94. K-520 (I) thru K-626
95. K-630 thru L-000 (S)

1880 CENSUS - INDEX
DEPARTMENT OF COMMERCE
BUREAU OF THE CENSUS

Explanation of Soundex Code. (Part-1)

Guide to the Soundex System

The Soundex filing system, alphabetic for the first letter of surname and numeric thereunder as indicated by divider cards, keeps together names of the same and similar sounds but of variant spellings.

To search for a particular name, you must first work out the code number for the surname of the individual. No number is assigned to the first letter of the surname. If the name is Kuhne, for example, the index card will be in the "K" segment of the index. The code number for Kuhne, worked out according to the system below, is 500.

Soundex Coding Guide

Code	Key Letters and Equivalents
1	b, p, f, v
2	c, s, k, g, j, q, x, z
3	d, t
4	l
5	m, n
6	r

The letters a, e, i, o, u, y, w, and h are not coded.
The first letter of a surname is not coded.
Every Soundex number must be a 3-digit number. A name yielding no code numbers, as Lee, would thus be L 000; one yielding only one code number would have two zeros added, as Kuhne, coded as K 500; and one yielding two code numbers would have one zero added, as Ebell, coded as E 140. Not more than three digits are used, so Ebelson would be coded as E 142, not E 1425.
When two key letters or equivalents appear together, or one key letter immediately follows or precedes an equivalent, the two are coded as one letter, by a single number, as follows: Kelly, coded as K 400; Buerck, coded as B 620; Lloyd, coded as L 300; and Schaefer, coded as S 160.

If several surnames have the same code, the cards for them are arranged alphabetically by given name. There are divider cards showing most code numbers, but not all. For instance, one divider may be numbered 350 and the next one 400. Between the two divider cards there may be names numbered 353, 350, 360, 365, and 355, but instead of being in numerical order they are inter-filed alphabetically by given name.

Explanation of Soundex Code. (Part-2)

Such prefixes to surnames as "van," "Von," "Di," "de," "le," "Di," "D," "Di," "dela," or "du" are sometimes disregarded in alphabetizing and in coding.
The following names are examples of Soundex coding and are given only as illustrations.

Name	Letters Coded	Code No.
Allricht	l, r, c	A 462
Eberhard	b, r, r	E 166
Engebrethson	n, g, b	E 521
Heimbach	m, b, c	H 512
Hanselmann	a, s, l	H 524
Henzelmann	n, z, l	H 524
Hildebrand	l, d, b	H 431
Kavanagh	v, n, g	K 152
Lind, Van	n, d	L 530
Lukaschowsky	k, s, s	L 222
McDonnell	c, d, n	M 235
McGee	c	M 200
O'Brien	b, r, n	O 165
Opnian	p,n,n	O 155
Oppenheimer	p, n, m	O 155
Riedemanas	d, m, n	R 355
Zita	t	Z 300
Zitzmeinn	t, z, m	Z 325

Native Americans, Orientals, and Religious Nuns

Researchers using the Soundex system to locate religious nuns or persons with American Indian or oriental names should be aware of the way such names were coded. Variations in coding differed from the normal coding system.

Phonetically spelled oriental and Indian names were sometimes coded as if one continuous name, or, if a distinguishable surname was given, the names were coded in the normal manner. For example, the American Indian name Shinka-Wa-Sa may have been coded as "Shinka" (S520) or "Sa" (S000). Researchers should investigate the various possibilities of coding such names.

Religious nun names were coded as if "Sister" was their surname, and they appear in each State's Soundex under the code "S 236." Within the State's Soundex Code S 236, the names are not necessarily in alphabetical order.

23, 1843. This date was only a year and a few months off from the information contained in the 1900 census. The one significant entry was the name of her father, John Keller,

SCHEDULE 1.—Inhabitants in _____, in the County of _____, State of _____,

enumerated by me on the 8ᵈ day of June, 1880.

	Stephenson James	w	m	26			Carpenter	England
	Henry	w	f	20		wife	Keeping house	England
	Edward	w	m	1		son	at Home	N.Y.
34	Griffin Patrick	w	m	60	father			England
	Mary	w	f	32		wife	Engineer	England
	Mair	w	f	19		dau	by	Ireland
35	Kruse Lewis	w	m	36			farmer	Denmark
	Louisa	w	f		wife	Home Keeping		Prussia
	Edward	w	m	1/2	son	at School		Denmark
	Lizzie	w	f	8	daughter		Home	Denmark
	Harry	w	m	2	son			N.Y.

1880 U.S. Census listing Lewis Kruse and Family.

which in turn meant that her maiden name was Marie Keller. I now had three great-great-grandparents to add to my chart. A thorough search of the Soundex for the 1880 census of the state of Massachusetts failed to turn up any trace of the Wild family. They certainly fell into the category of having children under ten, but to this day I have not been able to locate and trace them in the 1880 census.

I did have more success with the Kruse family using the method outlined, as it was a simple matter of breaking the name Kruse down into the Soundex code K-620. By checking the Soundex film rolls listed in the 1880 census manual, it was shown to be on roll 94. By searching the K-620 section under the name Louis, it wasn't hard to find the spelling "Lewis." The card indicated that the census schedule was in the Kings County section listed in enumeration district (E.D.) 118. It also indicated that the Kruse entry starts on sheet 30, line 13. By then referring to the schedule section, you can see that E.D. 118 is on roll 847. Could this be any easier? I have seen people struggle with this for hours, only because they hadn't done their homework.

As you can see, the schedule shows some new information. It shows "Lewis" and his wife, Lena, were then living at 96 North First Street in Brooklyn. They had a daughter named Lena who later became Lena Johnson. My grandfather John would not be born for another two years. To this day I have not found out what ever became of the other daughter named Lizzie.

It then occurred to me that perhaps the best source of information about the Kruse family might be found in Lutheran Cemetery. I wrote asking for a list of all the people buried in the Kruse family grave site. They replied promptly and explained that such a search would be time consuming and that the charge would be $30. The cemetery provided a list, which as you can see is quite detailed. No-

THE LUTHERAN CEMETERY
NON-SECTARIAN
— ∎ —
FOR PEOPLE OF ALL FAITHS

67-29 Metropolitan Avenue
Middle Village, N.Y. 11379

Telephones: (718)821-1750-1
Fax: (718)497-2750

September 18, 1992

Mr. Robert W. Marlin
P.O. Box 948194
Maitland, FL 32794-8194

Dear Mr. Marlin:

Below is a list of interments in Lot 11651 Map 3/A, registered owner Louis C. Kruse, deed dated October 23, 1877.

MARY B. KRUGER age 7 months, died 29 South Fifth Street, Brooklyn, buried August 21, 1875. Removed to this lot October 19, 1878.
CATHARINA KRUGER age 6 days, died 398 North Second Street, Williamsburg, buried August 22, 1876. Removed to this lot October 19, 1878.
LOUIS KRUSE age 2 years 2 months 3 days, died 35 Third Street, New York City, buried October 19, 1878.
LOUIS H. KRUZA age 3 years 2 months, died 866 Ewes Street, Brooklyn, New York, buried December 31, 1881.
HANNA KRUSE age 1 year 2 months 12 days, died 154 Tenth Street, Brooklyn, New York, buried November 26, 1885.
LENA KRUSE age 41 years, died 438 Keap Street, Brooklyn, New York, buried December 18, 1887.
ANNIE KRUSE age 6 months 6 days, died 438 Keap Street, Brooklyn, New York, buried June 23, 1888.
LOUISE C. KRUSE age 50 years, died 160 South Third Street, Brooklyn, New York, buried September 8, 1893.
WILLIAM JOHNSON age 6 years 14 days, died 142 Richardson Street, Brooklyn, buried July 21, 1896.
MARGARET JOHNSON age 25 days, died 14 Herbert Street, Brooklyn, New York, buried March 21, 1898.
KENNETH F. KRUSE (Ashes) age 35 years, died Ridgewood, New Jersey on April 26, 1990, buried June 6, 1990.

The variation in the spelling of the family name is taken from original book records. No other information is available.

Very truly yours,

Daniel C. Austin
President

Letter from Lutheran Cemetery listing gravesites in the Kruse family plot.

Death Certificate of Lena Kruse

tice the various spellings of the name Kruse. This is the way
the information was spelled on the original death certificates
and therefore could not be changed, even though it was
known to be incorrect. Other than Louis and his wife, Lena,
all the others were children who died in their first few years

of life. It later turned out that Lena had a total of eleven children. Only three of them lived past 1900. William and Margaret Johnson were the children of Lena Kruse Johnson the eldest daughter of Louis and Lena.

This list did give me enough information to send for a death certificate for Lena Kruse. I decided to go all out and order a death certificate for each of the children in the hope that something unexpected would show up. One surprise derived from the death certificates, which is not apparent from the cemetery list, is that two of the children, Louis and Catherine, were twins. How so? Count back six days from August 22, 1876. Then count back two years, two months, and three days from October 19, 1878. They were born on the same day—August 16, 1878—ergo, twins. There was no sign of my grandfather's brother Fred.

When these death certificates arrived, they added little to what I already knew. The exception was the death certificate of Lena Kruse, which listed when she had moved to the city of Brooklyn, as well as when she came to America. She died on December 18, 1887. Her death certificate showed that she lived in the city of Brooklyn for thirteen years and in the United States for thirty-nine years. (Incidentally, Brooklyn at that time was a separate city and did not become part of New York City until 1898.)

This means that the Kruses moved to Brooklyn in 1874. If they moved between December 18 (the day of her death) and the thirty-first of December, then you must add a year and come up with 1873. That is a possibility, but not a probability. By studying the death certificate of Mary B. Kruger, it is possible to speculate with a little more accuracy. Mary died on August 21, 1875. She was only seven months of age at the time, which would place her date of birth at about November 21, 1874. The death certificate shows that she had lived in Brooklyn since birth, which clearly places the Kruse

family in Brooklyn in 1874. Here I must give some credence
to the statement Lena Kruse Johnson made about living in
Manhattan as a young girl. All of this information led me to
a detailed study of the 1850, 1860, and 1870 censuses.

As stated earlier, nothing in genealogy ever happens in a
precise, logical, orderly, or chronological manner. You must
be prepared to go back and forth as necessary in order to
find what you want. And it doesn't always come easy. It was
at this point that I decided to get out of step and pursue the
mystery of what had happened to my grandfather's brother
Fred. The only information I had was what my mother remembered being told. He had been alive when she was
born because my mother remembered having contact with
his son Fred Jr., who was a year younger than she was. This
meant that Fred Sr. was probably alive as late as 1907, the
year my mother was born. He must have died sometime before my mother was seven in 1914, or else she would remember him. All I had to do was research the eight years
between 1907 and 1914. I started with death indexes and
found nothing even resembling the name Fred Kruse.

New York Times Indexes

The next step was the various *New York Times* indexes.
These include the Obituary Index, the Personal Surname
Index, and the General Index. They cover the years from
1851 to the present, and are one of the most overlooked
sources of information I know of. Many researchers ignore
the *Times*, thinking that since it is national in scope, it is too
snobbish to contain information about ordinary people. This
belief does have a certain truth to it. The *Times* Obituary
Index is usually available in the reference section of most libraries. It comes in two bound volumes. The first volume

covers the years from 1858 to 1968. The second volume covers the years 1969 to 1978. It is also true, generally speaking, that the index does cover mostly prominent people. But many researchers are not aware that the *Times* accepts both paid and unpaid obituaries and that the Obituary Index only covers unpaid obituaries, which are chosen as needed by the editors of the paper. They report on these deaths according to the prominence of the person and how much space they need to fill up the page on that particular day.

In the course of using it over the years, I have come across names like George Patton, Amelia Earhart, and Sara Bernhardt. However, I have also found names like Leonard Boudin, David Summerfield, and David Melnick, all of whom were distant relatives of mine. I never knew any of them personally, yet each of them was considered prominent enough to be included in these volumes. My point is that you never know where your next research lead is coming from. Don't overlook any source.

The paid obituaries are the ones that contain the names of millions of ordinary people. However, they are not indexed. You must know at least the month and year the individual died in order to access the material. For example, if you know the month and year a person died it is only necessary to check through the microfilm for that month and year. A month of microfilm for the *Times* is usually contained on three to five rolls of film. Just start with the first of the month. Not there? Just fast-forward the film to the next day. Using this method, one can zip through a month of the *Times* in less than twenty minutes.

However, a couple of additional things need to be mentioned. What if a person died within the last couple of days of the month? Then you must also search the first few days of the following month. There are two major exceptions: the months of June and August. The 4th of July and Labor Day come into play. Depending upon what day of the week they fall on, it may be necessary to check several additional days into the new month for these two months. It is not always easy to get a paid obituary inserted immediately for many reasons, including family grief, method of payment, and time.

The next index is the Personal Surname Index, which comes in two sets of alphabetized volumes. The first set covers the years from 1851 to 1974, and the second set covers the years from 1975 to 1989. In theory, these volumes contain the names of everyone mentioned in *Times* articles during any given year. Here again, the more recent years certainly deal with more prominent people. However, this was not always the case. In the earlier years, the *Times* reported on street brawls in Manhattan as well as petty thefts. They covered wife beaters and ladies who had been arrested for prostitution. In addition, they published daily those declaring bankruptcy as well as those being sued for nonpayment of debt. This tabloid type of reporting continued until the late 1930s. Therefore, when using these indexes from before that point, you never know with any certainty what information you'll find on any given name. It is certainly worth checking.

The General Index consists of thick volumes that theoretically contain reference to everything that appeared in the *Times*. This index is in bound volumes that begin with September 1851 and continue to the present. The very early years are sometimes bound with a number of years in one volume. Later on, a single year in a volume was divided into quarterly sections with each section having its own pagination. If you look up a name in the Personal Surname Index and it refers you to IV, 181, this means that you will find the entry in the General Index, October—December section, page 181. The General Index also has thousands of entries for people who are not listed in the Personal Surname Index. For example, they have a comprehensive section dealing with accidents. Listed are accidents that have occurred throughout the world; accidents that have occurred within the United States; accidents that have occurred in New York State; and accidents that occurred in New York City. This is further broken down into the boroughs of Manhattan, Brooklyn, Queens, the Bronx, and Staten Island. There are drowning accidents, automobile accidents, falling accidents, and train and bus accidents. The various cross-references are almost endless.

This is where I eventually found Fred Kruse, or Frederick Krauss, as the name was spelled in the newspaper account of his death. Everything my mother had related was quite

BROOKLYN CITY DIRECTORY

Louis Christian Kruse

Year	Occupation	Address
1875/76		29 South 5th Street
1876/77	Dockbuilder	388 North 2nd Street
1877/78	Ships Carpenter	35 South 3rd Street
1878/79	Dockbuilder	35 South 3rd Street
1879/80	Dockbuilder	35 South 3rd Street
1881/82	Dockbuilder	337 North 2nd Street
1882/83	Clerk	366 1/2 Ewen Street
1883/84	.	366 1/2 Ewen Street
1884/85		480 North 2nd Street
1885/86	Rigger	154 Keap Street
1886/87		154 Keap Street
1887/88	Rigger	438 Keap Street
1888/89		438 Keap Street
1889/90	Rigger	438 Keap Street
1890/91	Laborer	438 Keap Street
1891/92	Framer	438 Keap Street
1892/93		341 Ewen Street
1893/94	Rigger	160 North 3rd Street

Brooklyn City Directory listing Louis C. Kruse 1875/76 to 1893/94.

correct. He was driving some sort of hearse, which was hit by a trolley car. The news article also gave two reasons why I hadn't found any record of a death certificate. I had checked various spellings of the name Kruse, but Krauss was not one of them. Also, I had become careless with my search methods. In checking the Obituary Index, I had only covered the boroughs of Brooklyn and Manhattan. Both the accident and resulting death had occurred in the borough of Queens. This type of oversight is a classic example of what the expression "Attention to Detail" means. When checking out a lead, do it thoroughly. Don't take shortcuts. The one thing you don't check will contain the information you are looking for. It is "Murphy's Law" in action. When I was originally checking the death records, it would have taken only another five minutes to check the other two boroughs.

When I did receive Fred Kruse's death certificate, the best help it offered was his age, which was thirty-one. This made the year of his birth either 1879 or 1880. Because he was not included in the 1880 census, it is safe to assume that his birth occurred sometime after the census was taken. It turned out to be August 3, 1880. Even though Fred was not named on his birth certificate, all the necessary information was there to confirm that he was the right one. This baby boy was the seventh child born to Lena "Bennett" and Louis Kruse. They then lived at 66 New Hope Street. Later research showed it to be North First Street before it was renamed. It gave the birthplace of both parents as Germany. Lena was thirty-five and Louis was thirty-seven. These figures agree with the ages given on the birth certificate of my grandfather John two years later. The occupation of Louis was listed as dock builder.

Up to this time, I had not bothered to trace the Kruse family through the city directories. This was my next project and proved to be fairly easy. As far as I can tell, Louis C. Kruse

FRED KRAUSS WILL DIE

As Result Of Horrible Collision Between Car and Gig.

BODY OF INFANT THROWN TO ROADWAY FROM VEHICLE MONDAY NIGHT.

Two Men, Chas. Cassetto and Frederick Krauss, Were Taking Remains of Infant to Rooms of Brooklyn Undertaker.

While Charles Cassetto, of 721 Manhattan avenue, Maspeth, and Frederick Krauss, of 390 of the same thoroughfare, were driving a two-wheel cart owned by John Schlitz & Son, undertakers, of Brooklyn, along Jackson avenue, near Steinway avenue, about 5:45 o'clock Monday night, the cart was struck by a trolley car.

The impact threw both Cassetto and Krauss from the vehicle, also a box containing the remains of five-weeks-old Blanche Roller, of 21 Anderson avenue, Woodside.

The collision attracted a large crowd and for a time, when it was learned that the body of the child in its box had been also hurled to the street, pandemonium reigned.

The horse was almost instantly killed by the collision and the gig was wrecked beyond repair.

When Ambulance Surgeon MacTiernam, of St. John's Hospital, arrived, he worked over both men with the assistance of the ambulance driver, Terrence Smith, for nearly a half hour. Then, realizing that Krauss could not be benefited much by treatment, under the circumstances he ordered Patrolman William F. Burke, who had summoned him, to clear the way for the removal of both men to the ambulance, a short distance away. This was done under trying circumstances.

When the hospital was reached Dr. MacTiernam, after a minute examination, found that Cassetto was suffering from concussion of the brain and other injuries.

Krauss was found to be in a very critical condition, having sustained many injuries, including a fractured skull.

His fracture, according to Dr. MacTiernam, is an unusual one. Instead of being at the base of the brain, it extends from an eye backward. There is continual hemorrhage from the ears and his death is momentarily expected. He was alive and conscious, however, at press hour. His wife only last week went under a severe operation in a Manhattan hospital and she has not been apprised of her husband's condition.

Cassetto's condition is not as serious. If erysipelas does not set in his chances for recovery are good.

The two men were engaged under the order of the Coroner to take the body of the babe Roller from its home to the undertaking rooms of Schlitz & Son.

There was a widespread report, when the accident occurred, that there was some mystery about the case, in view of the fact that the child's body was in the gig. As a result ambulance chasers were in evidence and they worked on that supposition until nearly 10 o'clock today.

DIED AS RESULT OF COLLISION.

Frederick Krass, thirty-one years old, a driver, of 390 Metropolitan avenue, Brooklyn, died in St. John's Hospital, Long Island City, on Wednesday, from injuries received on Monday night while driving a wagon at Jackson and Steinway avenues, Long Island City. Krauss with another man had been to Woodside after the body of a child, and it was while taking the body to Brooklyn that a trolley car struck them. He received a fracture of the skull and nose and internal injuries, from which he suffered paralysis. Krass was employed by City Undertaker John Schlitz, of Metropolitan avenue, Brooklyn.

CAR HITS DEAD WAGON.

Body of a Child Spilled Into the Street and Driver Mortally Hurt.

An undertaker's wagon belonging to John Schmitz of 714 Metropolitan Avenue, Williamsburg, in which the body of a dead child was being conveyed from Corona to the undertaker's place of business, was struck in the side by a northbound trolley car at the junction of Steinway and Jackson Avenues, Long Island City, late last night. The wagon was smashed completely, the horse killed, and the driver, Frederick Krauss, and his helper, Charles Cassetta, were pitched to the sidewalk. The dead child was thrown with the coffin basket into the street.

Both Krauss and Cassetta were unconscious when picked up by passengers of the car, and had to be taken to St. John's Hospital, Long Island City, where the former was found to have a fractured skull. He has little chance of recovery. His helper was badly injured about the head and body, but will get well. The child's body was taken to the Steinway Police Station. No arrest was made.

Newspaper accounts of the death of Fred Kruse.

was a man who spent a good part of his life working with wood and ships. As you can see, all of the various occupations recorded relate to the trade of carpenter. Almost without exception, the various addresses given in the death certificates can be matched to one or more of the vital records I already had. The next step was to see if it was possible to go farther back from this time period.

CHAPTER 5

Marlin's Census Without the Soundex Method

A t this time I updated my chart and started to add some dates. As you can see, it had started to fill in nicely. It now included the names of five of my sixteen great-great-grandparents. It was about this time in my research that the 1910 federal census was released to the public. This release was met with mixed reviews. One of the problems was that only selected states and areas within them had been Soundexed. However, it did include all of those who had immigrated after the 1900 census.

By now I had made several thorough searches of the 1900 Soundex looking for my grandmother Hilda and my grandfather Meyer. I was assuming that both of them were already in America by 1900, but I had not found any evidence to confirm this. Suddenly it hit me like a lightning bolt why I hadn't been able to find my grandmother Hilda.

I was looking in the wrong Soundex code. I was looking under Korris, when I should have been looking under Kuraris. The double r in Korris is counted as one. Thus Korris

ANCESTOR CHART

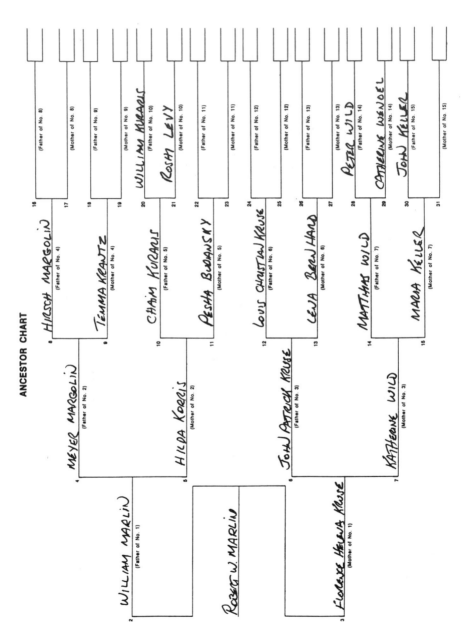

Ancestor chart—partially filled in.

1900 U.S. Census listing Beckie, Rosie and Hilda Koraris with Libby Summerfield's family.

becomes K-620. However, the double r with the vowel between them is a double six. I should have been looking
under K-662. My clue was in the spelling of the family name
on the passenger list when her father arrived. He and his
sons had arrived under the original family name of Kuraris.

All this was verified almost immediately. Within a day, I
had not only found my grandmother in the 1900 census, but
also two of her sisters, an aunt, and three other cousins. The
schedule showed that Hilda and her two sisters, Rose and
Beckie, were living at 244 Monroe Street on the Lower East
Side of Manhattan. They were shown as boarders at the
home of a lady named Libby Summerfield, who had three
children of her own—Rachael, David, and Pauline. In the
census schedule, grandmother's name was spelled Koraris.
It also listed her year of immigration as 1894. Her sister Rose
had also arrived in 1894 and her sister Beckie in 1899. As I
later learned, Libby Summerfield was Hilda's aunt. She was
the sister of my great-grandmother Pessie. Her Hebrew
name was really Pesha. The English version of Pesha was
Pauline. Pauline Summerfield was named after Pesha, who
had died some years earlier. Now I knew for certain why
Hyman and his boys had come to America without her.

It was also at this time I discovered that there was a way
to obtain information from federal censuses that had not yet
been released to the public. I sent a request to the Bureau
of the Census in Pittsburg, Kansas, asking for a copy of the
1920 federal census schedule for Meyer and Hilda Margolin.
They replied by sending the proper forms for submitting my
request. For a nominal fee they would search both the 1910
and the 1920 censuses and supply me with a complete transcript of all the information found. Considering that neither
of these censuses was due to be released to the general public for several more years, this was wonderful news. The

cb   5-068-9382

UNITED STATES DEPARTMENT OF COMMERCE
Bureau of the Census
Washington, D.C. 20233

October 25, 1979

OFFICE OF THE DIRECTOR

Re: Meyer and Hilda Moris Margolin

Robert W. Marlin
P.O. Box 1014
Great Neck, NY 11023

The following information, including spelling of name, relationship, age, etc., is an EXACT COPY
of the census record as reported by the census taker on the original schedule.

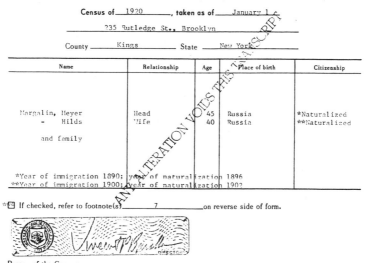

Census of ___1920___, taken as of ___January 1___

___235 Rutledge St., Brooklyn___

County ___Kings___ State ___New York___

Name	Relationship	Age	Place of birth	Citizenship
Margalin, Meyer	Head	45	Russia	*Naturalized
- Hilda	Wife	40	Russia	**Naturalized
and family				

*Year of immigration 1890; year of naturalization 1896
**Year of immigration 1900; year of naturalization 1902

*☐ If checked, refer to footnote(s) ___7___ on reverse side of form.

Bureau of the Census

The above information is furnished in accordance with title 13, United States Code, section 8.

The Bureau of the Census does not issue birth certificates, but this record is often accepted in place of one.

Transcript of 1920 U.S. Census listing Meyer and Hilda Margolin.

only thing I had to do to get what I wanted was to supply
copies of the death certificates of both grandparents.

Four weeks later I had the information in my hands. As
you can see, once again I hit pay dirt. Note that the name is
misspelled, but everything is there. The transcript of the

1920 schedule showed that Meyer immigrated to America in 1890 and had been naturalized in 1896. Hilda immigrated in 1900 and was naturalized in 1902. The address at 235 Rutledge Street was also new. A footnote indicated that this same address had been checked in the 1910 census, but no information had been found. This was a clue that I did not understand at the time. It became obvious that the Bureau of the Census has a way of checking through the 1910 index even in areas that were not Soundexed.

Sometime later while doing census research at the Federal Archives in Bayonne, I looked over at the other side of the room where microfilm was neatly stored in metal cabinets. It occurred to me at that moment that every bit of information that was possible to uncover in the 1910 federal census was right there, and that it was possible to find that information with or without the Soundex index. It was at that time that I started to develop a method, which I jokingly refer to as "Searching the census sans Soundex" or searching the census without Soundex. In case you are not familiar with the word "sans," it is French for without. I developed my method after the 1910 census was released. It was my answer to not having a Soundex index to work with.

To get started it was necessary to do a small amount of census history homework. Each time the federal census was conducted, New York City, like every other area of the United States, was broken down geographically into several levels of smaller units. The smallest unit and the only one we are now interested in is called the enumeration district or E.D. With some exceptions, many of these units not only numerically follow each other but also do so geographically. There is a method to the way the numbers of the E.D.s ran, as well as to their geographical use. However, the E.D. numbers as well as the size and shape of the E.D. changed from census to census. You cannot use the E.D. number found in the 1910 census to locate someone at that same address in the 1920 census.

There are two important items recorded in the 1910 census schedules that are usually disregarded or sometimes overlooked. It is these two items that are key to my method. In the schedules, the *street name* and *house number* appear on *each and every page.* You can be certain that the men who organized all this had no idea that including this information would aid in genealogical research more than seventy years later. To them it merely represented a fairly well-organized effort to count everyone in a concise and orderly manner.

My system is simple: First of all, it is important to know the exact street address of the family you are looking for. Then you must be able to locate the streets that border that address. The procedure is somewhat like plotting coordinates on a map. At the time the 1910 census was released the only street address I knew of was 287 Henry Street. This address appeared in two places. It was first listed as the destination address on the passenger manifest when my grandmother returned from Russia. The same address was on my father's birth certificate when he was born on February 10, 1910. If they were living at this address when the census was taken, all I had to do was find that address in the census. Using the street address of 287 Henry Street as a focal point, I then consulted several modern New York City street maps. They showed that Henry Street was only seven or eight blocks long. It ran between East Broadway and Madison Street. The street number of 287 was located between Scammel and Grand Streets. This breakdown of house numbers can be found in most cross-reference telephone directories.

In any case, that is how I located someone the first time I used my method of searching the census sans Soundex. In my example, I have used real locations and real people who

HENRY ST

231 Chase Robert .... RPub
231 Hayper S .... W2 OR ch 4-5846
232 Heyman M Dr .... dntst DR yd 4-8686
232 Shesfer Saul Dr .... off DR yd 4-1807
235 Block J .... OR ch 4-2409
235 Entel Harris .... SO OR ch 4-4550
235 Galuboff Julius .... W2 OR ch 4-9232
235 Sharasnof N .... W1 DR yd 4-1447
238 Rubin Jacob .... candy W1 DR yd 4-9595
239 Link Louis .... RPub
239 Ross Sam .... rustrnt S1 OR ch 4-8946
241 Karp Pauline .... OR ch 4-5932
241 Weinstein Ida Mrs .... DR yd 4-6232
242 Block John Dr .... DR yd 4-8660
242 Dolovof Sam .... S1 OR ch 4-7918
242 Rieger E Gerson .... DR yd 4-9097
249 Menaker M .... drugs DR yd 4-7719

MONTGOMERY   250   381

250 Golden Bros .... rustrnt DR ch 4-1596
253 Noshkin Rachmenioth Soc ... S2 OR ch 4-5407
255 Wax Rose Mrs .... OR ch 4-5996
256 Hochberg H B Dr .... WO OR ch 4-3345
256 Listebin Max .... OR ch 4-1737
256 Weinstein M ...... iro worts SO OR ch 4-5583
258 Itzion Needlewk Guild ...... W2 OR ch 4-6973
258 Mason Robt .... S3 OR ch 4-0286
259 Fuctovsky Israel Pincus Rabbi . OR ch 4-1668
262 Hebrew Day Nursery of N Y . OR ch 4-5262
263 Boruson Sam .... loncho OR ch 4-7652
264 Jacobs Evelyn .... OR ch 4-6837
264 Lovine J .... OR ch 4-5143
265 Henry St Settlement .... OR ch 4-8200
265 Nurses Settlement .... OR ch 4-8200
265 Visiting Nurse Service Henry St
        Settlement Henry Center OR ch 4-8200
265 Wald Lillian D Miss .... OR ch 4-8200
268 Wolpin Morris ...... grocw WO DR yd 4-7179

GOUVERNEUR   274

N Y City of PS 147 .... OR ch 4-2983
274 Drangle Danl .... S1 DR yd 4-0444
274 Hengiess Sam .... OR ch 4-7096
274 Mintz O .... SO OR ch 4-7432
274 Prylunt E L .... S2 OR ch 4-5732
274 Ruswick A .... DR yd 4-5944
274 Tick's Dairy & Groovy .... W1 DR yd 4-8421
278 Tepper Abr .... andy DR yd 4-9690
280 Cohen Gussie Mrs .... OR ch 4-7962
280 Gold Philip .... SO DR yd 4-2355
280 Israel C Z Mrs .... W1 OR ch 4-6237
282 Smith L .... S2 OR ch 4-0798
284 Coniuk I .... extm tlr SO OR ch 4-5988
284 Davis S .... OR ch 4-1907

SCAMMEL   287

287 Basmorind S Rabbi .... S2 DR yd 4-5643
287 Bloom Essie Miss .... OR ch 4-3752
287 Friedman Benj .... ogrs SO DR yd 4-7281
287 Ochs David .... W2 OR ch 4-7252
287 Tendler Isaac Rabbi .... S2 DR yd 4-5643
287 Weinstein Betty Miss ...... DR yd 4-8742
291 Charvinsay Benj .... WO OR ch 4-6228
291 Karins Wm Dr .... DR ch 4-3713
292 All Saints Church .... SO DR yd 4-1498
292 Rockwell Harrison Rev ... study DR yd 4-1498
295 Swift Leona Mrs .... RPub
296 Dalton Virginia M Miss .. W1 OR ch 4-0048
296 Gallagher John Jr .... OR ch 4-9027
296 Munca A .... WO DR yd 4-6073
297 Berger Emil .... WO OR ch 4-1498
297 Frantel M .... OR ch 4-4667
297 Gorden Saml .... OR ch 4-4236
297 Memorial Heatg & Coal Saving Serv
                       SO OR ch 4-1196
300 Bender Tillie .... OR ch 4-0121
301 Bloom Gussie Miss .... RPub
301 Henry St Settlement .... OR ch 4-8583
304 Heidazevch Helen V .... OR ch 4-7935
305 Bland Harry .... S2 OR ch 4-8924
305 Greenblott D .... RPub
305 Hoyley Karl D .... OR ch 4-0954
306 Drisonli Jos .... S1 DR yd 4-3175
308 Gorznlich Max .... DR yd 4-6458
313 Yonnes M .... W2 OR ch 4-1296
313 Maher Nellie .... W2 DR yd 4-7763
317 Falk J .... WO OR ch 4-1139
323 Hersum Hat Co .... OR ch 4-1678
324 Export Clthg Co .... OR ch 4-0560
326 Richter Henry .... W2 OR ch 4-0768
328 Boruson Abr .... OR ch 4-1654
330 Arendes Grocery Corp ... SO DR yd 4-4037
336 Adesso Luciano ..... rlstnry DR yd 4-9174
336 Karschinsky G ...... rustrnt DR yd 4-9738
336 Neborhood Elec Co ...... S2 OR ch 4-1387
336 Scheffer Isidore .... OR ch 4-7395
336 Spalline Phillip J .... W1 DR yd 4-4566

GRAND

Map of Lower East Side of New York City.

happened to have lived in New York City. The method described can be used anywhere. I have also used it for places like Buffalo, New York, and Philadelphia, Pennsylvania. In addition, I used it successfully to locate the family of a cousin whose relatives were from the more rural area of

Henderson, Georgia. It isn't always easy. The real secret is in doing your homework by learning just a little about the geography of the area you want to search. Doing this homework and expending the effort is *only important if you want to find what you are looking for.*

Census Research

The 1900 census schedules for all of New York County, which includes both the boroughs of Manhattan and the Bronx, are recorded on a total of fifty-three rolls of microfilm. The area I wanted to search was geographically located in a small area of downtown Manhattan known as the Lower East Side. Even though this was one of the most populated areas of New York County, it would have been impossible for it to take up more than ten rolls of film. Therefore, it was possible to eliminate the search of more than forty rolls. Already, the search was narrowed down.

There was one other thing that was unique to this area. All the streets and avenues had names rather than numbers. Just a short distance north of this area most streets and avenues were numbered. All of this area could also be eliminated. Starting with roll 996, I quickly established that it contained addresses in lower Manhattan. I skipped to roll 1,000 and found that the addresses were also south of the street area I was searching for. Now I did a roll-to-roll search. Roll 1,008 was the winner, leading me directly to 287 Henry Street. Just finding the address was a thrill, but I didn't find my grandparents! Instead, I found my grandmother's brother Abe Korris. He was listed as a merchant running a candy store. This was the first time I had located anyone in a census without using the Soundex. Since then, I have used this method hundreds of times and I've successfully located dozens of pieces of information that provided more information to continue my research.

Enumeration district indexes are also available for many areas on microfiche, which enables you to look up a street address. This in turn will tell you within which E.D. that street address is located. It is then a simple matter to scan through that E.D. until you are able to pinpoint what you are looking for. This is great until you must start researching an area whose E.D.s are not on microfiche. Also, I have found numerous errors in these E.D. indexes. In some cases the street addresses and numbers shown in the microfiche index are simply not part of the E.D. referred to on the microfiche. When this occurs I go back to my own previously stated method. Incidentally, this method can also be used for the 1900 census and the 1920 census if you don't have quick access to Soundex indexes.

An example of not having quick access to Soundex indexes occurs where I live. The Orange County library system, which also serves the city of Orlando, has what I consider one of the finest genealogical reference departments in this country. For a city of its size, Orlando outshines many major cities. The good news is that this library has on-site all U.S. Census schedules from 1850 to 1920. The bad news is that although this facility has the census schedules for all of these years, it does not have the Soundex indexes to readily access them. Considering the cost, it is easy to understand why. Perhaps it would be appropriate to point out that many major cities do not have the entire U.S. Federal Census for these years on hand. The city of Orlando had made a decision that I personally think was a stroke of genius. Knowing that they couldn't afford both the census schedules and the Soundex index, they chose to provide their patrons with the census schedules, based on the fact that the Soundex microfilm was available through the Family History Center at the Latter Day

DEPARTMENT OF COMMERCE AND LABOR · BUREAU OF THE CENSUS

THIRTEENTH CENSUS OF THE UNITED STATES: 1910 POPULATION

ENUMERATED BY ME ON THE _____ DAY OF _____

1910 U.S. Census listing Sam Katz and family and Abraham Korris.

Saints Church. For a nominal fee of $3 per roll, you can order the Soundex film you want from their headquarters in Salt Lake City. They then ship it to the branch of the church closest to you. It normally takes about two weeks for the film to arrive. When it arrives, you can use their facility free of charge to look up the enumeration district sheet and line number. Then it is a simple matter of using that information to locate and obtain a copy of the complete census schedule from the Orlando Library. This is a somewhat roundabout method that does work, but it takes an inordinate amount of time. Because of the delay I use my method almost exclusively.

There is one additional important item to be mentioned. When you do use my method of searching, don't forget to make a permanent note for future reference as to exactly where you made the find. Even if you don't find what you are looking for, it isn't a bad idea to make notes as to what street names and house numbers appear on the film reels that you scan through. In my case, Abraham Korris was living at 287 Henry Street, which was located in E.D. 94 of New York County, film reel 1,008. For each reference, it is a good idea to include the sheet and line numbers. At a future date when you might be looking for anyone else in that area, this would be your starting point. The same principle applies to any other area you might have to search.

On the surface, being able to locate my grandmother's brother probably doesn't seem to be too exciting, but what I was able to uncover as a result of that discovery is where the real fun and excitement in genealogical research begins.

So far I have only mentioned federal censuses. In addition to these, many states in the country have also conducted censuses of their own. Very few of these state censuses are as thorough or as comprehensive as their federal counterparts. They were generally conducted midway between federal censuses. For example, there was a New York State census taken for the years 1855, 1865, 1875, 1892, 1905, 1915, and 1925.

However, many of them are not easily accessible to the general public. Some of these state censuses are available on microfilm through the Family History Center at the Latter Day Saints Church. By using my method it is also possible to find families using these censuses, as long as you know the addresses they lived at when the census was taken. The 1892 and 1925 New York State census for Kings County (borough of Brooklyn) are currently available at the county clerk's office either by mail or in person. In either case you must know the street address in order to proceed. If you are out of town, the current cost is $10 for each address checked. When looking for state censuses, it is best to first check the film catalog at the Family History Center. After finding Abraham Korris at 287 Henry Street in the 1910 federal census, it was now my intent to check that same address for my grandfather Meyer in the 1905 New York State census. According to the passenger manifest, that was his address in May of 1906.

Within two weeks, I held in my hand a transcript from the 1905 New York State census. To say that I was surprised and delighted would be an understatement. Actually, I think the word flabbergasted would be appropriate. As you can see, the information it provided for me was astounding.

Basically it shows that my grandfather had a sister named Bertha who was married to Samuel Katz. They had five children. In addition to my grandfather, there was also a nephew named Harry living with them. This indicated that Meyer and Bertha had a brother, whose son Harry had been named after their deceased father, Hirsch. It also spelled the name wrong again. This time it matched the spelling on Hilda's passenger manifest. In addition, it gave everyone's age, relationship to the head of the household, and where they were born. If born out of the United States, it listed the

COUNTY CLERK, NEW YORK COUNTY
60 Centre Street, New York, N. Y. 10007   Fee Paid $1.00

No.   5218   EXTRACT OF STATE CENSUS

COUNTY CLERK—NEW YORK COUNTY

STATE OF NEW YORK   } SS.:
COUNTY OF NEW YORK

I, NORMAN GOODMAN, Clerk of the County of New York, DO HEREBY CERTIFY that I have examined the copy of the State Census, New York County, filed in my office and that the information given below is a true EXTRACT therefrom:

RE: _Meyer Margolies_ ___ ADDRESS _287 Henry Street_ _____ COUNTY OF NEW YORK As of June 1, 1905

FAMILY NAME	FIRST NAME	RELATION	COLOR	SEX	Age At Last Birthday	NATIVITY	Years In U. S. A.	Citizen or Alien
Katz	Samuel	head	w	m	37	Russia	15	al
	Bertha	wife	w	F	36	Russia	12	al
	Sarah	daughter	w	F	14	Russia	12	al
	Lillie	daughter	w	F	10	U. S.		at
	Harry	son	w	m	8	U. S.		at
	Morris	son	w	m	6	U. S.		at
	Jacob	son	w	m	5	U. S.		at
Margolies	Meyer	brother in law	w	m	38	Russia	12	al
	Harry	nephew	w	m	15	Russia	1	al

IN WITNESS WHEREOF, I have hereunto set my hand and affixed my official Seal

A.D. 4
E.D. 13   this_____30__day of _October_____ 19 81.
Page   1-4
94   _Norman Goodman_
                                      County Clerk, New York County

NOTE: THE SPELLING OF NAMES, ETC., IS AN EXACT COPY OF THE RECORD.

1905 New York State Census listing the Samuel Katz family along with Meyer and Harry Margolies.

number of years in America. Everyone was listed as an alien except the children who had been born here. The most recent arrival was Harry, who had arrived just the year before. This was a bonanza that I hadn't expected.

One of the first items I sent for was a copy of the passenger arrival list for Harry. At that time the chief source of indexes for passenger arrival information was the Passenger Arrival Records Division of the National Archives. It was only necessary for me to fill in as much information as possible on their form NATF 40 and wait two or three months for their report, which was usually negative. Over the years I have submitted this form at least forty or fifty times. Only once were they ever able to locate a passenger list for me. Finding the passenger list for Harry Margolin was no exception. In a later chapter, I'll show you how to circumvent some of the bureaucratic red tape.

The state census information opened up several other areas of speculation. Obviously, this census must have occurred while my grandmother was in Russia preparing to return with her father and brothers. Why had she remained there so long? When she returned to America the passenger list showed her son Sam's age to be what looked like 11 months old. That was in May of 1906. That would mean that Sam was born in Russia about June of 1905, which in turn means that he was conceived about September of 1904. Why she spent so much time there I may never know. For some time I thought it may have been to care for her mother. That her sister Rose named a daughter Pauline when she was born in 1903 made that theory fall apart. Children were only named after people who were already deceased. This is still somewhat of a mystery that may never come to light. On grandmother Hilda's death certificate, it listed my uncle Paul as the informant and recorded his address in 1962 as 195-08 Carpenter Avenue in Hollis, Queens. By checking with the Land and Title Transfer Office, I was able to learn the name of the attorney who handled the transaction. The attorney still had his office in Queens, so I decided to give him a call. It took several days to muster up the courage to call. This call might produce the first direct contact with an immediate family member. The thought of this made me extremely nervous. The possibility always existed that I was only an embarrassment whom they didn't want to hear from.

ORDER AND BILLING FOR COPIES OF PASSENGER ARRIVAL RECORDS	Please follow instructions below. Submit a separate set of order forms for each passenger arrival. Do not remove any of the sheets of this 3 part set. You will be billed $3.00 for each list reproduced. Do not mail payment with your order. This form will be returned to you and serves as your bill when we fill your order.	Date received

Mail the complete set of this order to ▶	Passenger Arrival Records (NNCC), Washington, DC 20408

IDENTIFICATION OF ENTRY

DATE OF ARRIVAL	NAME OF IMMIGRANT OR NAMES OF MEMBERS OF IMMIGRANT FAMILY	AGE	SEX
PORT OF ENTRY			
WHERE NATURALIZED (if known)			
SHIP NAME (or carrier line)			
PASSENGER'S COUNTRY OF ORIGIN			

NOTE

The National Archives has customs passenger lists dating back to 1820 with a few as early as 1787. Lists prior to 1820 that are not at the National Archives may be on file at the port of entry or the State archives in the State where the port is located. The Morton Allan Directory of European Passenger Steamship Arrivals may be useful in determining the name and arrival date of ships arriving at New York, 1890—1930, and Philadelphia, Baltimore, and Boston, 1904—1926.
Please fill in as much of the information called for above as possible. We will advise you if the information is inadequate to enable us to locate the entry you are seeking.
We do not maintain a list of persons who do research for a fee; however, many researchers advertise their services in genealogical periodicals, usually available in libraries.

YOUR NAME & ADDRESS	DO NOT WRITE BELOW - SPACE IS FOR REPLY TO YOU

PRESS HARD · Type or print legibly
Name · Number & Street · City & State

	ARRIVAL DATE	PORT	SHIP
☐ THIS IS YOUR BILL RECORD ENCLOSED ▶	MICROFILM PUBLICATION		make check or money order payable to NATF (NNCC)
	ROLL	PAGE	AMOUNT DUE ▶ $

☐ WE WERE UNABLE TO COMPLETE YOUR ORDER RECORD SEARCHED FOR BUT NOT FOUND ▶	RECORDS SEARCHED		
☐ SEE REVERSE	MICROFILM PUBLICATION		SEARCHER
	ROLL	PAGE	DATE SEARCHED

☐ A SEARCH WAS NOT MADE FOR THE REASON INDICATED:

☐ 1. Our index to New York passenger arrivals covers the periods 1820 – 1846 and 1897 – 1943. We regret that we cannot undertake a page-by-page search of the lists for the period between 1847 – 1896, inclusive.

☐ 2. Masters of vessels departing from U.S. ports were not required to list the names of passengers. Therefore, we would not have a list for the passenger you have cited.

☐ 3. Our holdings of passenger lists do not include any for Pacific coast ports. The San Francisco passenger lists were destroyed by fires in 1851 and 1940. (Consult the two works by Louis J. Rasmussen, San Francisco Ship Passenger Lists, 4 vols., 1965; and Railway Passenger Lists of Overland Trains to San Francisco and the West, 1 vol., 1966.)

☐ 4. Overland arrivals into the U.S. from Canada and Mexico are not documented in passenger list records.

☐ 5. Justice Department restrictions prohibit us from making searches in Immigration and Naturalization records less than 50 years old. We suggest that you direct an inquiry to: District Director, Immigration and Naturalization Service, New York, NY 10007.

(Zip code)

NUMBER OF BLANK ORDER FORMS YOU WOULD LIKE SENT TO YOU ▶

NATIONAL ARCHIVES TRUST FUND BOARD   NATF FORM 40 (12-79)

National Archives Passenger Arrival Form NATF 40.

I reached him on my first try. I identified myself and explained why I was calling. He obviously knew the entire family for some years, as he remembered the "boys" when they were quite young. He seemed somewhat aloof and volunteered nothing, but seemed to answer direct questions with direct answers. He told me that Sam had been dead for a number of years and that Paul had died in 1975 in California. He wasn't sure about Ruth and asked me if I had been in touch with Ted. When I explained that I had no idea where he lived, he volunteered something for the first time. The last he had heard, Ted was in the Navy and lived in Jacksonville. I thanked him and went directly to the library. In just a few minutes I found what I was looking for in the Jacksonville, Florida, phone directory.

After thinking the matter over, I decided to call Uncle Ted. If his response to my call indicated that the call was unwelcome, then I would not pursue the matter any further, thus avoiding embarrassment for both of us. I placed the call and spoke to him. Naturally, he was surprised to hear from me, but he was cordial. He did mention that his sister, Ruth, had moved to Jacksonville, but had passed away several years ago. I deliberately kept the phone call brief and told him that I would write to detail the information I was looking for. In less than a week I received his answer. Two things in his letter intrigued me. One was the mention of my grandfather having a brother in Buffalo. Could this be Harry Margolin's father? The other was the mention of a previous marriage and the existence of a half brother. After another quick phone call we agreed to meet the following weekend.

We got together twice on Saturday and once on Sunday. In spite of the fact that they welcomed me warmly and treated me very nicely, I felt ill at ease. I thought that perhaps it was because of my role as a "seeker of truth." Maybe this made my motives somewhat suspect. The issue of Jewish heritage was never really discussed in any depth. I'm still not certain whether or not Ted's children were aware that their grandparents were Jewish, and during our conversation I hinted that this possibility existed. No one seemed to pick up on my comment, that is, until his youngest son got me aside later and privately asked me a direct question. He

August 4, 1979

Dear Robert,

I recieved your letter and am amazed at the method you used to find us. I really can't tell you much because my father died when I was about five years old. I know about you because I remember Bill talking about you many years ago. It was even hard to remember even after you called on the phone. When I was at home Bill wasn't there much. When he was I was to young for him to talk to. You didn't tell us much about your family but I will tell you a little about me and my family.

I have been married for 35 years and have 3 children. My oldest is married and lives in California, my daughter is married and lives here in Jacksonville, the youngest lives with us at this time. We raised our children in a christian way and we are all christians and my wife and I belong to the Baptist church. I'll be glad to answer any questions that you may have. We would also be glad to have you visit us. Deloris, my wife has a sick Brother in Tenn. and may have to go up there and take care of him and because of this we are planning to go that way over the labor day weekend and since you are leaving for England the following weekend your visit will have to be next week of the week after that. I did see your father before he died and he was having heart troubles at that time. I got to talk to him a few times after that but did not get the word he was died until later on.

I guess I am the only remaining one carrying on the name. Paul has a son by the name of Fred Margolin living in New York some where. As you can tell we were not a very close family. Everyone was gone by 1938 except me and I left in 1941 to join the Navy and didn't get back until my Mother died and haven't been back since. Ruth came here to Jacksonville so that we could be close and she only lasted 4 years.

Beyond my Mother and Father I know very little about my grand-parents except that they came from Russia. My Mother had abrother and sister that lived in N.Y. and my father had a brother in Buffalo. When I was about 13 or 14 we were visited by my half Brother from Philadelphia and that is when I found out my Father had been married before marrying my mother. I never saw him again nor do I know any thing else about the family.

I hope some of this helps and if you have any other questions let me know or save it until we can get together. I tried to find out your phone number so I could call you but I found out it is unlisted. You didn't tell us anything about your family so let us hear all about it.

I will be waiting to hear from you again soon so I will close for now.

Most sincerly,

Ted Margolin

Letter from Ted Margolin.

asked if, in the event our mutual grandfather had been Jewish, any of my research indicated that he may have been a
"Christian in the heart." In case you are unaware, a Christian
in the heart would be a person who practices Judaism for
political or other reasons, but secretly is a Christian. Historically, this has usually worked the other way around. For example, prior to being expelled from Spain in 1492, Jews
were forced to convert to Christianity. Thousands simply became "Jews in the heart." In any case, I politely explained
that I had no firsthand knowledge or information regarding
the beliefs of our mutual grandfather. I didn't have the heart
to tell him that my research indicated only that both of our
grandparents were practicing Jews. It was quite apparent
that this young man was extremely proud of his family's
Christian values. I certainly didn't want to shatter that pride.

Ted knew nothing about the relatives in Buffalo—no
names or dates or anything that might provide any research
leads. Nor did he remember the name of the half brother
from Philadelphia. This seemed strange as he was a teenager
at the time of the visit. On Saturday afternoon, we drove
over to visit with Ruth's husband, Earl, who lived several
miles away. Earl was cordial and presented me with the
original copy of one of my grandfather's inventions. Earl had
fond memories of my grandmother and also remembered
her as a sweet, gentle lady. We spent the afternoon together
and I haven't seen or heard from him since.

We spent Sunday morning together making small talk
without touching on any new information. I flew back to
New York in the early afternoon with mixed feelings. It
never even occurred to me that any of the information I had
been given was deliberately misleading.

Naturalization Papers

My next step was to check for naturalization records for the New York City area. Most of these records were housed at the Federal Archives in Bayonne, New Jersey. (Since then, that facility has moved to downtown Manhattan.)

There are two basic types of naturalizations: those that occurred prior to 1906 and those after 1906. It was during 1906 that naturalization first became a federal function. All future naturalizations then came under the jurisdiction of the Immigration and Naturalization Service.

Pre-1906 naturalization proceedings were handled in somewhat loose and slipshod ways. They could be held in any court and each court had its own rules regarding what the qualifications for citizenship were. It didn't take early immigrants long to learn this, and they flocked to courts that were the most lenient. During some periods of time and in some courts, it was necessary to file a Declaration of Intention several years before applying for what became known as the "final papers." The final papers were actually a Petition for Naturalization. The actual "paper" was a certificate stating that the individual was a citizen of the United States. It is the Declaration of Intention and the Petition for Naturalization that usually contain the information that a genealogist desperately seeks.

All of the pre-1906 papers were indexed according to the same Soundex code as the census. Within twenty minutes I had found a Meyer Margolin. I knew immediately it was the wrong one because of the birth and arrival dates. It just happened to be the same Meyer Margolin whose death certificate I had sent for in error when I started my research. I spent hours going through every variant spelling and Soundex encoding I could think of for the surname Margolin. While there, I did check other family names that had been mentioned to me. This included Isaac Segal, Louis Boudin, and numerous other potential family members. I made copies of any record I thought might be even remotely related. This type of gamble has paid off many times. *When in doubt, make a copy.*

Not easily discouraged, I returned early the next day prepared to go through all available records that related to post-1906 naturalization proceedings. During the morning I found several more entries involving the name Meyer Margolin, but each of them was unusable for numerous reasons. By late afternoon I was just about ready to give up, when the attendant brought out index cards from the United States District Court for the Eastern District of New York. These were alphabetical rather than Soundexed. As I flipped through them I didn't come across the name Meyer Margolin, but I did find the name Hilda Margolin. My first thought was, *It couldn't be.* But it was! The attendant brought out a thick book with all the original Petitions for Naturalization. Before leaving the archives that day I not only had a copy of the Petition for Naturalization, but also a copy of the Declaration of Intention for Hilda Margolin.

To even try to list all the information on these two pieces of paper would not serve any useful purpose. Anyone can see that the sources contained leads to dozens of other research sources. All I can add here is that "my cup runneth over."

Sample index cards from the Naturalization Index. Each one is a relative.

TRIPLICATE
(To be given to declarant)

No. 259461

UNITED STATES OF AMERICA

ha
DECLARATION OF INTENTION   2x 33085 270933
(Invalid for all purposes seven years after the date hereof)

STATE OF NEW YORK
EASTERN DISTRICT OF NEW YORK } ss:

In the .... Court
of .... UNITED STATES   BROOKLYN, N. Y. ......
at ....

I, ... HILDA MARGOLIN
now residing at .... 1705 Carroll St., Brooklyn .... KINGS .... NY
occupation .... housewife ...., aged .... 58 .... years, do declare on oath that my personal description is:
Sex .... female, color .... white ...., complexion .... light ...., color of eyes .... grey
color of hair .... grey ...., height .... 5 .... feet .... 3 .... inches; weight .... 130 .... pounds; visible distinctive marks
.... none
race .... Hebrew ....; nationality .... Russian
I was born in .... Korsin, Kiev, Russia ...., on .... December 15, 1878
I am .... widow married. The name of my wife or husband was .... Meyer
we were married on .... February 1903 ...., at .... New York, NY ....; she or he was
born at .... Minsk, Russia ...., on .... September 10, 1868 ...., entered the United States
at .... New York, NY ...., on .... 1893 ...., for permanent residence therein, and now
resident deceased Dec. 1936 in Bklyn, NY I have .... 5 .... children, and the name, date and place of birth,
and place of residence of each of said children are as follows: .... Samuel, January 22, 1905;
.... Paul, May 8, 1908; William, Feb. 16, 1910; Ruth, Jan. 22,1915;
.... Theodore, April 3, 1921. Samuel born in Russia and the other four in Brklyn, NY
.... Paul lives in Maspeth,LI and the other four live in Brooklyn,NY
I have .... not .... heretofore made a declaration of intention: Number .... on ....
at ....
my last foreign residence was .... Roslov, Russia ....
I emigrated to the United States of America from .... Hamburg, Germany ....
my lawful entry for permanent residence in the United States was at .... New York, NY ...., and now
under the name of .... Hilda Margolin ...., on .... June 2, 1906
on the vessel .... name unknown

I will, before being admitted to citizenship, renounce forever all allegiance and fidelity to any foreign prince, potentate, state, or sovereignty, and particularly, by name, to the prince, potentate, state, or sovereignty of which I may be at the time of admission a citizen or subject; I am not an anarchist; I am not a polygamist nor a believer in the practice of polygamy; and it is my intention in good faith to become a citizen of the United States of America and to reside permanently therein; and I certify that the photograph affixed to the duplicate and triplicate hereof is a likeness of me: So HELP ME GOD.

Hilda Margolin
(Original signature of declarant without abbreviation, also alias, if used)

Subscribed and sworn to before me in the office of the Clerk of said Court,
at .... Brooklyn, NY .... this .... 29th .... day of .... April
anno Domini 19 37. .... The photograph affixed to the duplicate and triplicate hereof is a likeness of the declarant.

Thomas Mackhusm
[SEAL] DEPUTY Clerk of the .... U S DISTRICT .... Court.
By ...., Deputy Clerk.

No. 42188

Hilda Margolin

Form 2202—L-A
U. S. DEPARTMENT OF LABOR
IMMIGRATION AND NATURALIZATION SERVICE

Declaration of Intention of Hilda Margolin.

Nationality Russian

ORIGINAL
(To be retained by clerk)

SS

No. 273933

UNITED STATES OF AMERICA

PETITION FOR NATURALIZATION

To the Honorable the ___ 2, District ___ Court of ___ Eastern District ___ at ___ Brooklyn, N.Y.

The petition of ___ HILDA MARGOLIN ___, hereby filed, respectfully shows:

(1) My place of residence is ___ 399 Troy Ave. Bklyn. NY ___ (2) My occupation is Housewife

(3) I was born in ___ Korsin Kliev, Russia ___ on ___ Dec. 15, 1878 ___ My race is ___ Hebrew

(4) I declared my intention to become a citizen of the United States on ___ Apr. 29, 1937 ___ in the ___ Eastern District ___ Court at ___ United States ___ at ___ Brooklyn, NY

(5) I am a widow. The name of my wife or husband was Meyer ___

we were married on ___ Feb. 1903 ___ at ___ New York, NY ___ he was born at ___ Minsk, Russia ___ on ___ Sept. 18, 1968 ___ entered the United States at ___ New York, NY ___ on ___ 1893 ___ for permanent residence therein. and now resides at ___ deceased Dec. 1908 in Bklyn, NY ___ naturalized on ___

at ___ certificate No. ___ I have ___ 5 ___ children, and the name, date, and place of birth, and place of residence of each of said children are as follows: Samuel–Jan. 22, 1905–Russia–Bklyn

Paul–May 8, 1908–Bklyn-Maspeth, LI

William–Feb. 16, 1910–Bklyn–Bklyn

Ruth–Jan. 22, 1915–Bklyn–Bklyn

Theodore–Apr. 3, 1921–Bklyn–Bklyn

(6) My last foreign residence was ___ Boslov, Russia ___ I emigrated to the United States of America from ___ Hamburg, Germany ___ My lawful entry for permanent residence in the United States was at ___ New York, NY ___ under the name of ___ Hilda Korris ___ on ___ 1893 ___ on the vessel ___ unknown ___

(7) I am not a disbeliever in or opposed to organized government or a member of or affiliated with any organization or body of persons teaching disbelief in or opposed to organized government. I am not a polygamist nor a believer in the practice of polygamy. I am attached to the principles of the Constitution of the United States and well disposed to the good order and happiness of the United States. It is my intention to become a citizen of the United States and to renounce absolutely and forever all allegiance and fidelity to any foreign prince, potentate, state, or sovereignty, of whom (which) at this time I am a subject (or citizen), and it is my intention to reside permanently in the United States. (8) I am able to speak the English language. (9) I have resided continuously in the United States of America for the term of 5 years at least immediately preceding the date of this petition, to wit, since ___ 1893 ___

and in the County of ___ Kings ___ this State, continuously next preceding the date of this petition, since ___ 1893 ___, being a residence within said county of at least 6 months next preceding the date of this petition.

(10) I have not heretofore made petition for naturalization No. ___ on ___

at ___ and such petition was denied by that Court for the following reasons and causes, to wit:

and the cause of such denial has since been cured or removed.
Attached hereto and made a part of this, my petition for naturalization, are my declaration of intention to become a citizen of the United States, certificate from the Department of Labor and the affidavits of the two verifying witnesses required by law.

Wherefore, I, your petitioner, pray that I may be admitted a citizen of the United States of America, and that my name be changed to ___

I, ___ HILDA MARGOLIN ___ do swear (affirm) that I know the contents of this petition for naturalization subscribed by me, that the same are true to the best of my own knowledge, except as to matters therein stated to be alleged upon information and belief, and that as to those matters I believe them to be true, and that this petition was signed by me with my full, true name: SO HELP ME GOD.

Hilda Margolin
(Complete and true signature of petitioner)

AFFIDAVITS OF WITNESSES

Bella Sachar ___, occupation Housewife & Saleslady
residing at ___ 611 Nostrand Ave. Bklyn, NY ___, and

Samuel L. Budinoff ___, occupation Retired
residing at ___ 865 Montgomery St. Bklyn, NY

each being severally, duly, and respectively sworn, deposes and says: I am a citizen of the United States; I have personally known and have been acquainted in the United States with ___ HILDA MARGOLIN ___, the petitioner above mentioned, since ___ Jan. 1, 1934 ___ and that to my personal knowledge the petitioner has resided in the United States continuously preceding the date of filing this petition, of which this affidavit is a part, to wit, since the date last mentioned and at ___ Brooklyn, NY ___ in the County of ___ Kings ___

this State, in which the above-entitled petition is made, continuously since ___ Jan. 1, 1934 ___ and that I have personal knowledge that the petitioner is and during all such periods has been a person of good moral character, attached to the principles of the Constitution of the United States, and well disposed to the good order and happiness of the United States, and in my opinion the petitioner is in every way qualified to be admitted a citizen of the United States. I do swear (affirm) that the statements of fact I have made in this affidavit for naturalization subscribed by me are true to the best of my knowledge and belief.

Bella Sachar
(Signature of witness)

Samuel L. Budinoff
(Signature of witness)

Subscribed and sworn to before me by the above-named petitioner and witnesses in the respective forms of oath shown above in the office of Clerk of said Court at ___ Brooklyn, NY ___, this ___ 2 ___ day of ___ May ___, Anno Domini 19 ___ 40 ___ 259461

Certificate of arrival No. ___ showing the lawful entry for permanent residence of the petitioner above named, together with Declaration of Intention No. ___ of such petitioner, has been by me filed with, attached to, and made a part of this petition on this date.

[SEAL]

___ Clerk
By ___ Deputy

No. 62846

Form 2204-L-A
U. S. DEPARTMENT OF LABOR
IMMIGRATION AND NATURALIZATION SERVICE

Petition for Naturalization of Hilda Margolin.

CHAPTER 6

Declaration of Intention
for Naturalization

A quick look at the Declaration of Intention and Petition for Naturalization for Hilda Margolin should give you some idea of how many new sources of information any document can produce. In this case the number is tremendous. Both of these documents will be discussed in detail in Chapter 8.

In an earlier chapter, I mentioned that I would explain why it is necessary to request a copy of the *original* document, instead of an extract, when ordering a marriage license. Here is a copy of the original of my grandfather's marriage license. It was passed on to me by Ruth's husband during my trip to Jacksonville. As you can see, if you compare it to the extract, it contains five items not mentioned in the extract. The first item it contains are names of both witnesses. They were Peter Boudin and Isaac Segal. It also named the rabbi, Meyer Budinoff. In addition, it listed the name and address of his synagogue. Notice any connections?

*Copy of front side of original Marriage License
of Meyer Margolin and Hilda Korris. (Part-1)*

*Copy of back side of original Marriage License
of Meyer Margolin and Hilda Korris. (Part-2)*

Meyer Budinoff was one of the witnesses when Rose Korris married Ike Segal. Was this the same Isaac Segal who married Rose? Who was Peter Boudin? Was there any connection between Rabbi Meyer Boudinoff, Peter Boudin, and Samuel L. Budinoff? Perhaps you noticed that Samuel L. Budinoff was one of the witnesses when my grandmother filed her Petition for Naturalization. The other was her sister Bella Korris Sachar. Lots of pieces of the puzzle were slowly coming together. As I pointed out earlier, neither the facts you uncover nor the ideas you come upon ever occur in any chronological order. As a matter of fact, they don't even occur in a particularly rational order. How you approach the research is unimportant as long as it works for you. The bottom line is how much information you can document, and how much you can add to your chart.

For example, at the moment I was savoring the find of my grandmother's "papers," I started thinking about finding her

Photo of headstone at gravesite of Libby Summerfield.

listed in the 1900 census as living with Libby Summerfield. Who was Libby Summerfield? It suddenly occurred to me that during my visits to the cemetery, I had taken a number of random photos of headstones in the United Friends and Relatives section. A bell was going off in my head reminding me that the headstone of Libby Summerfield was one of them. It took me only minutes to find the photograph. She had died on September 6, 1951, at the age of eighty-three. Naturally, the first thing I did was send for a copy of her death certificate.

By this time, patience was becoming somewhat of a virtue. I no longer haunted the mailbox or cursed the mailman when he failed to bring what I was waiting for. The death certificate of Libby Summerfield produced one surprise, which was that her maiden name was Boudinoff. Her father was Samuel Boudinoff and her mother was Rachael. As you can see, the death certificate did not contain her mother's maiden name. It suddenly occurred to me that perhaps Budiansky, Budinoff, and Boudin were just variations of the same family surname. This was only a speculation. If this was so, then Peter Boudin and Libby Summerfield were the brother and sister of my great-grandmother Pesha. This also meant that Peter was my grandmother's uncle and Libby was her aunt. As stated earlier, speculation is allowed as long as it is not recorded as fact on a genealogical chart. Sometimes it takes an overstretched imagination to be able to fit pieces of the puzzle together. As long as you can separate speculation from fact, you are still on the right track.

A Good Informant

My next step was to try to contact Libby's son David, who was named as the informant on her death certificate. A quick

Death Certificate of Libby Summerfield.

check of the 1900 census schedule showed that David had been born in 1893, so the possibility existed that he was still alive. A check of all the phone directories in the New York City area showed no listings for anyone with the surname of Summerfield. This was one of the cases where a quick check of the *New York Times* Obituary Index turned up what I was looking for. As you can see, he passed away in November of 1965. The obituary also mentions his widow and a sister

Obituary of David Summerfield from The New York Times.

named Rae Ellennoff, who lived in California. I was unsuccessful in finding his widow. A check of phone books on microfiche listed only one family named Ellenoff in the entire Los Angeles area. The lady who answered the phone was extremely nice and listened for several minutes as I explained the reason for my call. She waited until I was finished and then told me that I probably wanted to speak with her niece, Ruth Resnick, who lived in Oceanside, California, which is located between Los Angeles and San Diego. She even provided me with the phone number, which I called almost immediately.

Ruth Resnick turned out to be a walking, talking book of knowledge regarding the Budiansky family. Not only is her memory phenomenal, but her degree of accuracy is astounding. Her contribution to what you are reading cannot be measured. Many of her memories were ingrained by people, places, and events from the time of her early childhood in the 1930s, until the death of her grandmother Libby (Summerfield) in the early 1950s. Her mother was Rachael, Libby's oldest daughter. To begin with, she and I share mutual ancestors. There is Samuel Budiansky, who is Ruth's great-grandfather and my great-great-grandfather. My great-grandmother Pesha and Ruth's grand-mother Libby were sisters. A genealogical relationship chart shows us to be second cousins, one generation removed.

On the Trail of the Budianskys, Slutskys, and Melnicks

A good part of Ruth's knowledge of the Budiansky family came directly from her grandmother Libby or her own child-hood memories of people, places, and events. Her grand-mother's memories were my first direct link to the distant past. As I had suspected, there was a direct link between the names Boudin, Budinoff, and Budiansky. Some family mem-bers had changed their names from Budiansky or Budinoff to Boudin.

To begin with, Peter Boudin and Libby Budiansky Sum-merfield were brother and sister. They were just two of the ten children of Shmuel and Ruchel Budiansky who lived in Boslov, a city located about sixty miles southeast of Kiev in the Ukraine. The English translation of Shmuel could be Samuel or Solomon. Ruchel usually became Rebecca. There was at least one older son who did not immigrate to Amer-ica. He stayed behind to take over the day-to-day operations of his aging father's general store. Most of the daughters did immigrate to America. Taking into account Peter, Libby, my great-grandmother Pesha, and the unnamed son who stayed behind, this meant that there were at least six of the children who were not accounted for.

Ruth also had a vivid memory of Libby's sister Raizel, who was known as Rose, and whose married name was Resnick. She did not remember her uncle at all, which probably meant that he died prior to Ruth being old enough to re-member him. She did remember cousins who belonged to the Melnick family, the Slutsky family, the Bikoff family, and

several other families who may or may not have been related. This included the Coyne family and the Sunshine family. There was also a man named Ben Sloat who was married to someone in the Lerner family.

The information Ruth was able to provide seemed to be
endless. It sometimes came in small fragments, but almost
everything was totally accurate. You must remember that
this kind of information never comes to you in chronological order. Getting it all together is your job. Just be thankful
that someone takes the trouble to relate it to you.

Ruth later recalled other facts about the Resnick family.
They were also a large clan with somewhere between seven
and ten children. Most of the children had been born in Europe and had come to America as adults. One of the daughters was also named Rose. She had married a man named
Burkowsky or Borkowsky. Ruth had never had occasion to
see the name written, so the spelling was only an approxi-
mation of what she had heard. They had operated a news-
stand somewhere in New York City during the 1920s or
1930s.

There was a daughter named Pauline, who was very close
in age to Ruth's mother, which means that she had been
born about 1895. There was also a daughter named Ida,
whose married name was Jason. I recalled that the names
Pauline and Ida had appeared more than once in documents
I had compiled. It was my belief that these Paulines were all
named after my great-grandmother Pesha. However, I had
no idea who all the Idas were namesakes of. One of the
Resnick sons was named Abe and another was David. One
other item Ruth later recalled was that she thought that
Raizel had passed away sometime in the late 1920s. I'm sure
that by now you can guess that this afterthought was probably one of the most important pieces of information of all.

Ruth was equally informative with regard to the Slutsky family. They were also a large clan. The head of the clan was named Shaya, which was a Yiddish nickname. Ruth had no idea what his Hebrew or English given name may have been. Shaya was Libby's nephew. However, he was some years older than his aunt, which was a source of amusement for some family members. This disparity in age occurred because Libby was born late in Ruchel Budiansky's life. Ruchel was fifty when Libby was born. This is the sort of clue that a genealogist considers a jackpot bonus. Did you pick up on it? Since Libby was born about 1868, this set the birth year of Ruchel Budiansky at about 1818. My own experience has proved that it is rare to be able to pinpoint the birth of a great-great grandparent in this manner. If I could now pinpoint Ruchel's maiden name I might be able to add two more great-great grandparents to my chart. The only other information Ruth remembered on the Slutsky family was that Shaya had a daughter named Bertha, who had married a doctor.

Information on the other surnames was somewhat sparse. But Ruth believed that all of them were somehow related to the Budiansky family. Therefore, I decided that it was worth my time and effort to establish exactly how each was related. Even though they may not be direct-line relatives, the collected data could prove to be invaluable at some later date. Ruth remembered a lady named Jennie Sunshine, who had a daughter named Florence. She also mentioned a lady named Beckie Coyne. The only thing recalled about the Melnick family was that there had been a Dave Melnick who had been in the insurance business. Ruth was certain that all of these ladies were related to the Budiansky sisters who were not yet accounted for. However, she had no idea if the relationship was by marriage or blood. Establishing what these relationships were was my job. It was my feeling that I now had enough information to begin. My search started with the death certificate for Raizel Resnick. To be on the safe side, I started with the *New York Times* Obituary Index for the year 1934 and moved forward. Within fifteen minutes I had located what I thought was probably the right death certificate. Rose Resnick, age eighty-three, had died on April 20, 1943. She died in Manhattan and the certificate number was 8613. It was that simple. I immediately sent for the death certificate.

While I was waiting I decided to check the city directories for New York City to see if I could locate any information on Raizel's daughter, Rose Burkowsky. The earliest death certificate on hand at the Family History Center at the Latter Day Saints Church for the borough of Manhattan was for 1920. I found nothing under the spelling of Burkowsky or Borkowsky that made reference to a wife named Rose or being in the newspaper business. However, I checked Berkowsky and found a Nathan Berkowsky who had a news business at 362 West 42nd Street and resided at 362 West 42nd Street. Although it didn't mention a wife named Rose, this sounded like a good possibility.

Conjecture turned into near reality the next day when I was able to locate this family in the 1920 census schedules. This was done without the Soundex, using the method previously described. In any case, it showed that Nathan was married to a lady named Rose and that they had a son named Edward who was eight, and a son named Joseph who was two. Rose Berkowsky was thirty-five years old and had immigrated to America in 1900. This meant that she was born in 1885 and had immigrated to America when she was fifteen. Nathan had not immigrated until 1905, which indicated that they were married sometime after 1905. In spite of almost overwhelming evidence, I was not certain that these were the right people. Until I could document their relationship to the Resnick family, all of this was still conjecture.

1920 U.S. Census listing Nathan Berkowsky and family.

The following day I was back at the Family History Center checking New York City marriage indexes starting with the year 1905. A search that took ten minutes showed that a Nathan Berkowsky had been married on September 4, 1910, in the borough of Manhattan and the certificate number was 20326. A copy of this marriage license was immediately ordered and I moved on to other things.

There was little new information on the Wild family, and I was slowly becoming convinced that the marriage of Matthias and Maria must have taken place before they came to America. It was also my belief that Matthias had made a deliberate attempt to cover his tracks after leaving France. It is even my suspicion that his name was originally something other than Wild. When he was naturalized in 1883, he gave the date of his immigration to America as May 10, 1862. I searched every reported ship arrival manifest for the entire month of May 1862 and turned up nothing that even remotely resembled Matthias Wild. He gave his year of birth as 1845, which would have made him seventeen at the time, or very nearly draft age. The American Civil War was well under way by then and I'm sure the possibility of conscription would not have escaped him.

In the 1900 census, Matthias reported that he was born in January of 1840 and that both he and Maria had immigrated in 1870. It is my belief that this was closer to the truth. Without a date, however, finding him through a search of the passenger manifests would be impossible because those passenger lists are not indexed. In the 1920 census, taken while he was at the Kings County Home for the Aged, he gave the year of his immigration as 1873. Inasmuch as the Boston city directory first picked him up in 1874, this is a real possibility. A check of the index for Boston passenger arrivals showed nothing. It is my belief that he changed his name upon arriving in America. Without even a remote idea of when he arrived or what his original name was, I am going to have to come up with some creative solutions to solve this mystery.

My next search for him will be on the other side of the ocean, where I will visit his ancestral village of Soultz. It is my hope that I will be able to check his birth records, since he used two conflicting dates on legal documents. The 1900 census shows his birth date to be January of 1840 and his immigration papers show the birth date to be February of 1845. Somehow I don't think he lied about where he was born. With luck I may also be able to locate information about Maria, assuming she came from the same area. It is also my hope that they may have been married in his hometown. In the meantime, I have placed this matter on the back burner.

The Berkowsky marriage license arrived first. Now conjecture did turn into reality. Raizel Budinsky and Meyer Resnick were listed as the mother and father of the bride. The groom's parents were Isaac Berkowsky and Celie

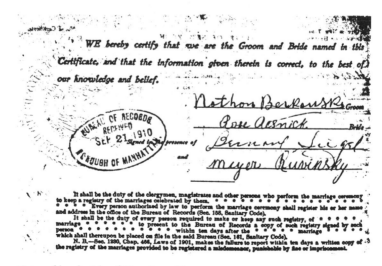

Copy of front side of Marriage License
of Nathan Berkowsky and Rose Resnick. (Part-1)

Copy of back side of Marriage License
of Nathan Berkowsky and Rose Resnick. (Part-2)

Kouter. There were also two surprises. One of the witnesses was Bernard Siegel, who was the brother of Ike Siegel. The

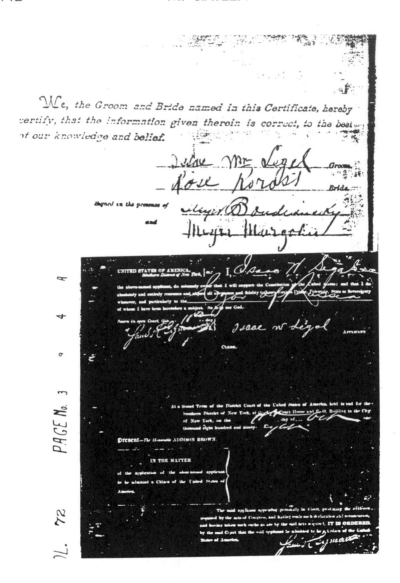

Signature comparison of Isaac Segal.
Top signature is from his Marriage License to Rose Korris.
Bottom Signature is from his Naturalization Petition.

rabbi was once again Meyer Budinoff. He seemed to be showing up everywhere. Although it has not been mentioned before, it should be obvious as to how important the signatures on these certificates can be for future reference and comparison. Here is an example. Take a good look at Ike Siegel's signature on his naturalization petition in 1898 and on his marriage license in 1902. See how easy it can be to accurately document your own genealogy? The death certificate of Rose Resnick also added much information. The first thing it did was add two more great-great-grandparents

Death Certificate of Rose Budiansky Resnick, wife of Meyer Resnick.
This is the mother of Rose Resnick Berkowsky.

to my chart. It also cleared up the mystery of who all the Ida's were named after. It was Itta Ruchel (Ida Rachael) Cohen, the wife of Samuel (Shmuel) Budiansky. Rose was a widow when she passed away, so if necessary it would not be difficult to locate the death certificate of her husband, Meyer. She is interred in Montifiore Cemetery. The informant was a daughter, Rebecca, whose married name was Schor.

Rose Resnick had married Nathan Berkowsky in September of 1910. The home address of the bride was listed as 340 East 4th Street in Manhattan. Once again, it was a simple matter to locate that address in the 1910 census. Voila! I now have a list of the entire Resnick family. Please note that at this time the family name was "Resnikoff." It occurred to me that it wasn't necessary to go any farther in order to complete my personal goals. I had already discovered the names of my great-great-grandparents for this part of my family. At this point, however, I made a decision to continue along this line to see how many of the Budiansky sisters I could find and document. As stated earlier, this extra information might prove helpful at a later date.

Now I turned my attention to the Slutsky family to see what I could uncover based upon the information I had. The only solid lead was Shaya, but first I had to find out what his given name really was. The first source I turned to was a volume in my permanent home library called, *The Complete Dictionary of English and Hebrew First Names* (see Appendix). Shaya was listed and defined as a short or pet form of the name Yeshava, which in turn was related to Isaiah. This could make the English version Isaac, Isadore, Issy, or even Ike.

It proved unnecessary for me to go any farther along this trail, as something happened that is an example of what I have been trying to point to as "attention to detail." Over a period of years every genealogist amasses information that seems to be unrelated to the search they are conducting. In my case all of

1920 U.S. Census listing the family of Meyer and Rose Resnick.

these notes, documents, and potpourri go into a file with the simple title of "Unrelated Miscellaneous Documents(UMD)."

At least once a month, I go through all the papers in this file checking and rechecking to see if any of this old information fits in with anything I've learned since the previous reading. This practice had paid off more than once. Some years before I had sent for a number of Budinoff birth certificates. All of these were instances where the child had been given the name Pauline or Pearl or any variant that might represent the name Pesha. My assumption was that the child may have been named after my great-grandmother and was therefore possibly related. One of the birth certificates in this file was for a Pearl Budinoff who was born in October of 1905 to Louis and Rebecca Budinoff. At that time I could not make a connection so it went into my UMD file. This time, though, I thought I spotted a solid connection. Rebecca Budinoff's maiden name was Slutsky. Could "Slugsky" possibly be a misspelling of Slutsky?

On one of my trips to the National Archives, I made copies of every pre-1906 naturalization petition I could locate under the name Budinoff or Boudin. A check of miscellaneous nat-

Birth Certificate of Pearl Budinoff.

Naturalization Index Card of Louis Budinoff.

uralization documents I keep on hand included one for a
Louis Budinoff who had been naturalized on April 2, 1901.
In spite of a two-year age difference that I ignored, I zeroed
in on the street address, which was 218 6th Street.

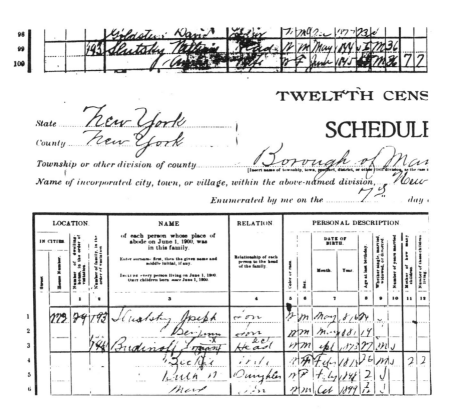

1900 U.S. Census listing William, Annie, Joseph and Benjamin Slutsky.

Using my "sans Soundex" method, I located that part of 6th Street at the very beginning of roll 1,087, which begins with E.D. 139. A search of the numbers on the even side of the street produced nothing. At number 223 on the odd side of the street you will see that Louis and Rebecca Budinoff are listed along with their daughter, Ruth, and son, Max. Now take a look at the four people entered on the schedule just before Louis. William and Annie Slutsky and their two sons, Joseph and Benjamin. Two separate households living at the same address. Was this just a lucky find? Or was it attention to detail paying off again?

My next bit of luck once again involved using a little bit of conjecture. There is little doubt that Rebecca Slutsky Budinoff was related to William and Annie Slutsky. How could I document all this? It occurred to me that both of the Slutsky sons were of marriage age in spite of the fact that both were currently living at home. Starting with the year 1900 I checked the marriage index for all five boroughs of New York City. Naturally, I checked all the spelling variations of the name Slutsky I could think of. For the year 1907 I found a Joseph Slutske in the Brooklyn index. He had been married on October 20, 1907, certificate number 7830.

My search continued up to the year 1915, but I found no entries for Benjamin Slutsky and no further entries for any other Joseph Slutsky. Perhaps it was time for a little more conjecture. Could the name Ben Sloat that Ruth mentioned have been an Americanized version of Benjamin Slutsky? It took no more than twenty minutes to locate a Ben W. Slote. This entry also appeared in the Brooklyn section of the same index. The marriage took place on July 15, 1907, the same year I found the entry for Joseph Slutske. Could both brothers have married within the same year? There was one sure way to find out. I immediately ordered copies of both marriage certificates.

The results follow for you to see. These two men are without any doubt the same Slutsky brothers listed in the 1900 census. Ruth was right even about Ben Slote marrying into the Lerner family. Wolf is the Hebrew equivalent of William, and Anna and Hannah are almost interchangeable. One brother gave his mother's maiden name as Budinoff, while the other gave it as Budiansky. Here was another sister. Also, don't overlook the rabbi who performed both ceremonies. None other than Meyer Budinoff. Is all this discovery a matter of luck? Is it a result of chance, or attention to detail? I'll let you be the judge. The bottom line is that you can attain the same results.

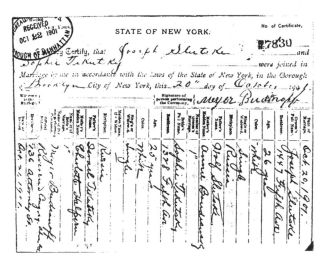

Marriage License of Ben Slote.

Marriage License of Joseph Slutske.

Finding the Melnick family was simply a matter of consulting a source described in detail earlier. It is the *New York*

July 1, 1955

DAVID MELNICK

David Melnick, a retired life insurance executive, died of a heart attack yesterday at his home, 800 Avenue H, Brooklyn. His age was 82.

Mr. Melnick was born in Russia. He was employed by the Prudential Insurance Company of America for, thirty-two years until his retirement in 1932. Mr. Melnick began as an agent and was a special assistant superintendent in Brooklyn at his retirement. He was a Mason.

Surviving are his widow, Mrs. Jennie Cigal Melnick, three sons, Maurice and Sidney of Brooklyn and Howard of Briarcliff Manor, N. Y.; three sisters, Mrs. Rebecca Coyne of the Bronx and Mrs. Jennie Sunshine and Mrs. Anna Ruskin, both of Brooklyn; two half-brothers, Philip Melnick of the Bronx and Dr. Harry Melnick of Florida, and seven grandchildren.

MELNICK—David, beloved husband of Jennie, devoted father of Sidney, Milton and Howard, loving grandfather and dear brother. Services today, 1 P. M., "Kirchenbaum's Westminster Chapels," Coney Island Ave. (Avenue H), Brooklyn.

Obituary of David Melnick from
The New York Times.

Times Obituary Index. Checking into the Obituary Index also cleared up some of the other loose ends. Beckie Coyne and Jennie Sunshine turned out to be sisters of Dave Melnick. Inasmuch as his wife's maiden name was Jennie Siegel, she was not a Budiansky sister. This probably meant that his mother's maiden name was Budiansky.

My approach to this situation was as follows. David Melnick was eighty-two when he died in 1955, which made his year of birth about 1873. Having no idea what the names of his parents were, I decided to zero in on the year of his marriage. Using the age of twenty as an arbitrary starting point, I began searching the marriage index beginning with the year 1893. The early indexes were not broken down by borough, but rather by month. Therefore, each year until the year 1900 required a search of all marriages for each month of every year. This search took less than an hour. In the year 1900 I found a David Melnick who was married in Manhattan on December 26, 1900. In spite of this find, I continued to search for

Marriage License of David Melnick and Jennie Siegel.

any other David Melnicks up until the year 1910. There were no others.

When the marriage license arrived it was all there. He was married to Jennie Siegel. His father's name was Hyman Melnick and his mother's name was Sarah Bodjansky. (This was another misspelling of the name Budiansky.) Another Budiansky sister found. But I didn't stop there. Using the 137 Suf-

1900 U.S. Census listing the family of Hyman and Sarah Melnick.

folk Street address, I searched the 1900 census and found the rest of the family. Now I even knew the month and date of Sarah Budiansky's birth. Once again, was it luck or attention to detail? To continue on this line, as it turned out, Shaya Slutsky's real name turned out to be Simon. His daughter Bertha did marry a doctor named Nathan Rachlin. In the final analysis, almost all of the information Ruth provided was totally accurate. I can't thank her enough.

CHAPTER 7

1920 Federal Census

At 9:00 A.M. local time on January 1, 1920, the United States Federal Enumeration began. By law, its contents were to remain sealed for seventy-two years. On May 2, 1992, the contents of this census were officially opened to the public for the first time. It was truly a bonanza for genealogists. Until this census was released, I was at somewhat of a standstill in parts of my research. This was especially true with regard to the Margolin portion. As mentioned, I had already gained access to the 1920 schedules for my grandparents, but the information contained did not uncover anything new or startling. I had researched the Sam Katz family and the only document I added was a copy of the birth certificate of Sylvia Katz who was born in 1909. It did confirm that her mother Bertha's maiden name was Margolin, making her a sister to my grandfather Meyer. I had run into a total dead end on their nephew, Harry Margolin. As the 1910 census showed, he was no longer living with Sam Katz. There were a number of Harry Margolins living in New York by then, but I found nothing to tie any of them in with

Birth Certificate of Sylvia Katz.

either my grandfather or the Katz family. I then checked city directories up to 1925, but found nothing.

By this time, I had acquired both a microfilm and a microfiche reader for home use. I had also become a member of the American Genealogical Lending Library. Provided with their yearly membership is a complete catalog of their extensive microfilm and microfiche collection. For modest fees one can rent all kinds of film and fiche that include everything from census schedules to passenger lists. It is a quick, convenient way to do research. Simply look up the film numbers and call in an order. Within a week the film arrives and you have more than a month to look it over. If you need something in a real rush, they are happy to ship via priority mail, in which case the order arrives within two days. Naturally, there is a charge for this service, but it is still a great arrangement.

When the Soundex for the 1920 census became available, I sent for the rolls containing Sam Katz and Harry Margolin. The Katz family was now living at 1575 Bathgate Avenue in the Bronx. Sam and Bertha ran a vegetable market. Two of the girls, Sarah and Lillie, must have gotten married. They were no longer living at home. Everyone else was still there, but just a little older. There were many Harry Margolins. I went through each one and compared the age and year of immigration contained in the 1905 New York State census. Only one of them matched. The next day I was able to get a copy of that schedule at the Orlando Public Library.

Back to Tracing the Margolins and the Kruses

The Harry I had picked out was twenty-eight years old and had immigrated to America in 1904. He was married to a lady named Bessie and had a son named Edward whose age was two years and one month. They were living with their brother-in-law, William Schlossberg, and his wife, Eva, and their daughter, Winifred. This also meant that Eva Schlossberg and Bessie Margolin were sisters. Harry and his wife both gave their birthplace as Minsk, Russia. It is unusual to see anything but a country listed in a census. They were married in 1918 and both were naturalized. Lots of new information! By the way, it is a good idea to remember that this census started on the first of January and therefore it was safe to add one year to any age found in the schedule. The age reported in the schedule is the age of the person as of January 1 of that year. In any case, where do I go from here?

After thinking about it for a while, it occurred to me that although Harry and his wife, Bessie, were most certainly long gone, their son Edward could still be alive. At my local

1920 U.S. Census listing Harry Margolin and family.

county library I checked through telephone books on microfiche for all available major American cities from Boston to Seattle to San Diego to Miami and back to Boston. This search took a number of hours. When it was over, I had the names, addresses, and telephone numbers of nine different men with the name of Edward Margolin. After thinking it over, I decided to write each a letter rather than call them on the phone. It took me several days to get the letter to-

```
                              P.O. Box 948194
                              Maitland, FL 32794-8194
                              3 September 1992

                              Telephone (407) 834-3037
```

```
Mr. Edward Margolin
   - - -
   - - -
```

```
Dear Mr. Margolin:
```

For the purpose of family genealogical research I am attempting to contact Edward Margolin who was born in the Bronx, NY sometime around December 1917. The Edward Margolin I am seeking is the son of Harry and Bessie Margolin. Harry was born about 1890 and immigrated to the United States around 1904. Harry was the nephew of my grandfather, Meyer Margolin. This makes Harry and my father William first cousins. Meyer's sister Bertha was married to Samuel Katz and they also lived in the Bronx.

I am seeking any available information which would enable me to continue my research. It is my hope that someone in the family may have passed on documents which might still exist. This could possibly be in the form of a marriage license, a birth certificate or naturalization papers.

If you have any information, or any suggestion as to anyone I might contact, I would certainly appreciate hearing from you. Many thanks for any help you might be able to offer.

```
                              Most Sincerely,



                              Robert W. Marlin
```

Copy of letter sent to Edward Margolin.

gether, but when I was finally satisfied that it was right, I entered it into my word processor and produced original copies of the same letter addressed to each one of the nine. I mailed these letters and went on to other things.

Progress on the research of my maternal ancestors was going very slowly. In spite of all the information I now had on the Kruse family, I had not been able to go back any farther on my chart. My great-grandparents, Louis Christian Kruse and his wife, Lena, were still almost a total enigma. Lena's death certificate indicated that they had moved to Brooklyn about 1874, and I was fairly successful in tracking them forward from that date. Going backward produced nothing. According to available documents, Louis was born about 1843, but there was nothing to indicate when he had immigrated, and to date I have not been able to locate a marriage certificate. As a matter of fact, I had invested more than $75 (at $3 per inquiry) having various spellings of the name Kruse checked in the marriage license index. The death certificate for Lena Kruse indicated that she was born around 1846, arriving in America in 1848 at the age of two. This meant that she should be listed under the family name of Bernhard in at least two censuses. The only thing I didn't have was the first name of her father, who would be listed as head of the household unless her mother was a widow.

My next step was to try some speculation. Louis and Lena had four sons. Two named Louis, one named Fred, and my grandfather, John. The names Louis and Fred were first names of other Kruse families listed in both censuses and city directories. Therefore, I reasoned that John Kruse may have been named after Lena's father. The 1850 and 1860 indexes had a number of entries for John Bernhard, John Bernhardt, John Bennet, and John Bennett. My search started by checking each one of them in the hope of locating a child named Lena who would have been four years old in 1850 or fourteen years old in 1860. To make a long story short, I have drawn a complete blank in this search.

Over the years I have spent countless hours searching the 1850, 1860, and 1870 censuses and found nothing. Compared to most later censuses, the information contained in them is extremely limited. In spite of this it is possible to make good use of the available data. A short description of their contents are in order. The 1850 census was the first one to list the name and occupation of each member of a household. Prior censuses listed only the name of the head of household. In addition, it gave the age, sex, occupation, and place of birth of each member of the household. Both the 1850 and 1860 census schedules were identical. The 1870 schedule also recorded whether or not the father and the mother were foreign born.

An index for the 1850 and 1860 census is available in book form at most libraries having a genealogical department. This same index exists for portions of the 1870 census, but is not available for all areas. At the present time there is no index available for New York City for the 1870 census. An index is available for the city of Brooklyn, which was not part of New York City at that time. The city of Brooklyn is indexed as part of Long Island. However, even the indexes that are available only list the names of the head of each household. Each head of household listed referred to a ward number and a page number. The ward is a political subdivision used in most major cities. The ward was further broken down into assembly districts and enumeration districts.

Inasmuch as I was now fairly certain that the Kruse family had moved to Brooklyn about 1874, it seemed reasonable that I might be able to locate them in the 1870 New York City census. In order not to miss anything, I had already checked the Brooklyn index thoroughly and eliminated all entries with a spelling anything like Kruse.

I found numerous entries in city directories for the name Louis Kruse. Each entry was checked out. None of those checked had any remote relationship or similarity to the Louis Kruse I am looking for. In the case of Lena Bernhard the same blank wall exists. The pronunciation of the name Bernhard in German can easily be mistaken for Bennet or Bennett. This spelling even appears on some documents. Not having any idea what the names of her parents may have been has made this a difficult problem.

I have not been able to locate birth certificates for Lena or Lizzie, the two Kruse daughters listed in the 1880 census. Of course, the registration of a birth was not always mandatory and even when it was many people didn't bother to do so. Some simply had a church baptism and let it go at that. It was also necessary for me to check all variant spellings of the name Kruse. To date I have found more than thirty. There are still several avenues that I have not yet explored. Several companies in Utah are currently preparing an index to the 1870 New York census. When this is complete it is possible that I might pinpoint either Louis or Lena and work from there.

The other possibility is to go to New York City and spend time at the municipal archives personally checking the marriage indexes from 1872 through 1874 for a marriage license for Louis and Lena. This covers the years when I believe the marriage occurred. All of the searching I have done in the past has been done by other people, because at the time these indexes were not available to the public for their personal use. This procedure changed several years ago when the records were transferred to the municipal archives. Any way I look at it, I am only one marriage license away from being able to document all four of my great-great-grandparents on this line. So you can see that although the problem is somewhat difficult, it is not insurmountable. Locating that single marriage license would provide me with the names of both of their fathers as well as the maiden names of both of their mothers.

Several weeks had passed since I mailed letters to each Edward Margolin on my list. I had enclosed a stamped self-addressed return envelope with each. Several were returned as having moved and the forwarding order had expired. Several others came back with comments like, "Wrong Edward Margolin" or "Not me" scribbled across them.

One evening the phone rang just as I was entering the front door. The woman on the other end of the line asked for me, and then she identified herself as Mrs. Edward Margolin of Scottsdale, Arizona, a suburb of Phoenix. She was the widow of Edward Margolin. He had passed away just a few years earlier. However, she was sure that all of the information in my letter related to his family. I had located the right Edward Margolin, but I was a few years too late. Then she said something that absolutely stunned me. She said, "By the way, have you been in touch with his sister?"

When I explained that I was not aware that a sister existed, she explained that Edward's sister, Leslie, had been born some years after Edward. This was why she was not listed in the 1920 census. Her name was Leslie Margolin Auerbach and she lived in Seattle. She also gave me her telephone number. I waited several days to call. The first time I called I got an answering machine and I hung up. Somehow I felt that I must speak with this woman directly.

Leslie was home the second time I called. She was expecting my call and was happy to hear from me. We chatted for several minutes before getting down to the nitty-gritty of who we were and from whence each of us had come. I told her about my father and she told me about hers.

About five minutes into the conversation each of us simultaneously said to the other, "My grandfather's name was Meyer." There was a full fifteen seconds of silence before each of us realized the truth. Meyer Margolin was the grandfather of us both. Harry Margolin was not Meyer's nephew, he was his son from a former marriage.

Over a period of weeks, Leslie and I attempted to piece together all the various parts of the overall story. Most of Leslie's information was passed on to her firsthand by her father and mother. Some of it was based on her own experience. Almost all of my contribution to the story was based on the information contained in the various documents I had amassed. We both believe our efforts are as accurate as possible.

Our mutual grandfather, Meyer, married Leslie's grandmother, Rose Rubin, sometime around 1890. Her father, Harry, was born about 1891. Meyer came to America about 1893, promising to send for his wife and son as soon as possible. More than ten years passed and nothing happened. At the turn of the century pogroms started again in Russia. (A pogrom was the organized persecution and massacre of Jews.) Numbers of Jews were being killed for no reason other than being Jews. Rose Margolin decided that to save her son she would send him to his father. It was 1904 and Harry was fourteen. Rose tied a tag around his neck, kissed him good-bye for the last time, and shipped him off to his father.

Harry arrived in New York Harbor on March 6, 1904, aboard the S.S. *Pretoria.* My research has shown that Meyer married my grandmother, Hilda, in January 1904. He must have still been on his honeymoon. Somehow, he had neglected to tell anyone that he was already married and had a fourteen-year-old son. He had also not bothered to obtain either a civil divorce or a "git" (Jewish divorce).

We can't even guess what went through his mind when he received notice that his son Harry was at Ellis Island waiting for his father to pick him up and take him home. Meyer's reaction was simple. He ignored the notice and left the boy sitting on a bench at Ellis Island. Finally, the responsibility of getting Harry fell on his uncle, Sam Katz. Neither Leslie nor I know what happened during that early period, or how Hilda, Meyer's second wife, reacted to the sudden appearance of Harry. It was not too much later that she returned to Russia to get her father and brothers. This also accounts for her absence during the 1905 New York State census. At this time both Meyer and Harry were listed as part of the family of Sam and Bertha Katz.

On the seventh of March, 1908, Harry enlisted in the United States Army. He became part of what was then called the White Field Artillery and spent most of his time in the Philippine Islands. He was discharged from the army on March 9, 1911, when his enlistment expired. After leaving the army he had little, if any, contact with his father. Leslie said he seldom spoke about him, but obviously he harbored a lot of animosity.

Because of Leslie's interest I decided to pursue some of the new leads she had provided me. I was able to obtain a complete copy of her father's service record. I made a copy and presented it to her as a tribute to her father. I ordered several rolls of passenger arrival index films in the hope of locating Harry's passenger arrival record.

In addition to the passenger index for Harry Margolin, I ordered several others, including the Budinoff index and the Koraris index. This is when I discovered why reports on these indexes so often come back negative. While going through films, it became quite apparent that whoever had filmed the original index cards had done a terrible job. There were large sections containing hundreds of entries

THE UNITED STATES OF AMERICA.

STATE OF .... **NEW YORK,**

CITY, TOWN, OR MILITARY POST } **FORT SLOCUM.** } *ss:*

I, _Harry Margolin_, born in _Berlin_, in (See Instruction 2.)

the State of _Germany_, aged _20_ years and _1_

months, and by occupation a _Driver_, DO HEREBY ACKNOWLEDGE

to have voluntarily .... enlisted this .... **10** .... day of .... **MAR** ...., 190_8_,

as a *soldier* in the ARMY OF THE UNITED STATES OF AMERICA, for the period of *three years* unless sooner discharged by proper authority: And do also agree to accept from the United States such bounty, pay, rations, and clothing as are or may be established by law. And I do solemnly swear (or affirm) that I will bear true faith and allegiance to the *United States of America;* that I will serve them honestly and faithfully against all their enemies whomsoever; and that I will obey the orders of the President of the United States, and the orders of the officers appointed over me, according to the Rules and Articles of War.

(See Instruction 2.) _Harry Margolin_ .... [SEAL.]

Subscribed and duly sworn to before me this _10_ day of .... **MAR** ...., A. D. 190_8_,

.... Captain, Med. Dept., U. S. A.

Recruiting Officer.

I CERTIFY that I have carefully examined the above-named man agreeably to the General Regulations of the Army, and that, in my opinion, he is free from all bodily defects and mental infirmity which would, in any way, disqualify him from performing the duties of a soldier.

.... Captain, Med. Dept., U. S. A.

Examining Officer.

I CERTIFY that I have minutely inspected the above-named man, _Harry Margolin_ previous to his ...... enlistment, and that he was entirely sober when enlisted; that, to the best of my judgment and belief, he fulfills all legal requirements; and that I have accepted and enlisted him into the service of the United States under this contract of enlistment as duly qualified to perform the duties of an able-bodied soldier, and, in doing so, have strictly observed the regulations which govern the recruiting service. This soldier has _blue_ eyes, _brown_ hair, _ruddy_ complexion, is _5_ feet _4 1/2_ inches high.

.... [SEAL.]

.... Captain, Med. Dept., U. S. A.

Recruiting Officer.

U.S. Army Enlistment Papers of Harry Margolin. (Part-1)

NOTE.—Indelible or permanent marks found upon the person: _Scar 2 & left elbow. Back = scar 1" black. Scar 1/2" left lower back. Scar 1/2" left lower middle finger._

CONSENT IN CASE OF MINOR.

(See A. R. 862.)

I, ... do certify that I am the .... of .... ; that the said .... is .... years of age; and I do hereby freely give my consent to his enlisting as a soldier in the United States for the period of three years.

Given at .... this .... day of ...., 190 .

Witness:

This applicant was accepted for enlistment on the .... day of ...., 190 , by ....

Captain, Med. Dept., U. S. A.

Recruiting Officer.

w-19

DECLARATION OF APPLICANT.

(See Instruction 3.)

I, ... desiring to enlist in the Army of the United States for the term of three years, do declare that I have neither wife nor child; that I am of the legal age to enlist, and believe myself to be physically qualified to perform the duties of an able-bodied soldier; and I do further declare that I am of good habits and character in all respects and have never been discharged from the United States service (Army or Navy) or any other service on account of disability or through sentence of either a civil or military court, nor discharged from any service, civil or military, except with good character, and for the reasons given by me to the recruiting officer prior to this enlistment.*

AND THAT I AM A CITIZEN OF THE UNITED STATES.

Given at Fort Slocum, N. Y.

this .... day of ....

Witness:

*Here add, in case of an applicant for first enlistment: And that I am, or have made legal declaration of my intention to become, a citizen of the United States.

Residence of applicant:

Name and address (street and house number, if any) of person to be notified in case of emergency, giving degree of relationship; if friend, so state:

.... enlisted at Fort Slocum, N. Y., on the .... day of ...., 190 , for Mounted Service, White, Field Art'y.
by Capt. LeWald, Med. Dept., U. S. A.

(Arm of service or organization. See instruction 2.)

.... enlistment; last served in ....

Discharged ...., 190 .

INSTRUCTIONS.

1. One enlistment paper only will be made in the case of a soldier enlisted or reenlisted for the Army. It will be forwarded directly to The Adjutant General of the Army, with the recruiting officer's tri-monthly report. The enlistment paper of a noncommissioned staff officer serving at an indeterminate post will, however, be forwarded to the commanding officer of the post.

2. The recruiting officer will enter in the appropriate place the arm of service or organization in which the soldier was enlisted, e. g., in cases of enlistments for staff corps, "Post Noncommissioned Staff," "Hospital Corps," "Signal Corps," "Ordnance Corps," or in cases of enlistments for general service, "Mounted Service, white," "Mounted Service, colored," "Foot Service, white," "Foot Service, colored," adding the more definite designation "Engineers," "Cavalry," "Field Artillery," "Coast Artillery," or "Infantry," as the case may be.

3. The correct name of the recruit will be ascertained. The Christian name will not be abbreviated, but if it consists of more than one name, only the first will be written and signed in full. Great care will be exercised that the name is correctly written and signed wherever it appears on the enlistment paper.

4. In cases of reenlistment, i. e., enlistment within three months from date of last discharge from the Army, the prefix "re" will be added to the word "enlisted" in other respects as in the case of a first enlistment. If an applicant for reenlistment is a married man the declaration of applicant is to be amended by lining out the words "I have neither wife nor child" and adding on the blank lines following the declaration a note showing the conjugal condition of the applicant, and number of children, if any.

Assigned to ....

of ....

RECEIVED
ADJUTANT GENERAL'S OFFICE
MAR 14 1908
U. S. A.

U.S. Army Enlistment Papers of Harry Margolin. (Part-2)

that were totally blank, or so light that it was impossible to make out even the surname. Thus, when you receive the report on a search of the arrival index, it simply states "not found." It does not state that the portion of the index searched may be illegible. Therefore, if you can establish a date of arrival, it is important to check the arrival schedules directly if you can't find the information you want in the indexes. This is tedious and time consuming and *only important if you want to find what you are looking for.*

I found nothing for Budinoff or Koraris, but I found Harry in no time at all. Not only was it there, but it was neatly typed and totally legible. I still can't account for the fact that several years earlier the National Archives had searched this same index and found no record of him. It once again proves that you shouldn't accept negative reports as the final word. Either check the same information several times, or take the time to check the information yourself.

The index showed Harry had arrived in America on March 6, 1904, on board the S.S. *Pretoria.* It then gave a reference as to where the complete schedule could be found. A copy is included here. In spite of the usual errors the basic information is correct. Note that Meyer's address is given as 141 Monroe Street, which is the same address as that shown on his marriage license to Hilda.

The index did provide one unique piece of information, which is the name of the town he came from. We now know where it all started. Leslie also cleared up a mystery that had bothered me for some time. She remembered in some detail that as a child she had made several trips to visit Hilda some years after Meyer's death in 1929. When Harry went to visit Hilda, he was accompanied by his children, Leslie and Edward. We then realized that our uncle Ted's story about a half brother from Philadelphia was a fabrication. He just didn't want me to dig up too much of his past, by accident

PASSENGER AND IMMIGRATION LIST FOR HARRY MARGOLIN

Arrived New York on 6 March 1904 on S.S. Pretoria which left Hamburg, Germany on 19 February 1904.

PASSENGER LIST

Hirsch Margolin   Age 13   Laborer   From Bobrysh
To be met by father Chaim Margolin-141 Monroe Street NYC

Traveling with:

Meyer Platkyn   Age 25   From Bobrysh
Traveling to Philadelphia-Kriozar-730 N. 2nd Street. Was returnd
to medical division for illness developed during the trip.

IMMIGRATION RECORD OF DETAINED PASSENGERS:

Group 25 List 78 #341 Margolin, Hirsch Father: Meier 370 East 4th St.
Group 27 List 4 #342 Plastyn, Meyer Friend: Meier Margolin

Arrived on 6 March 1906. Released at 3:00 P.M. By Immigration

1 Meal (Lunch)

Because of the poor quality of the microfilm, it was impossible to make a photocopy of the original document. The information shown above was copied exactly as it appeared in the original document.

Passenger Arrival Record of Harry Margolin.

or design. All of those trips to Philadelphia and the countless hours of research were all in vain. That half brother he spoke of was from the Bronx, not Philadelphia! Leslie remembered that her mother, Bessie, encouraged the visits, although she was not certain about the reason. She thought it might have been so that Harry would not be estranged from his half brothers, although by that time, most of them were married and not living at home.

It took me a long time to get over the anger I felt toward my uncle Ted for leading me on a wild-goose chase. But it taught me a good lesson. Don't accept anything as gospel until you check it out and document some of the facts. Without finding anything I should never have devoted that much time to any one lead. Also, remember that even a family member is quite capable of outright deception if they feel threatened by what you might uncover.

It is my belief that my father, William, never knew that he had a half brother. By the time Harry made his trips to Brooklyn, Paul and my father had both married and left home. My uncle Sam knew, but I have no idea whether they stayed in touch. Leslie described her father as a warm, loving man who constantly reminded his little girl of how much he cared for and appreciated having her as a daughter. Her warm descriptions of him made me somewhat envious.

It was at this time that I realized that with one exception I had uncovered as much information as I could on this side of the Atlantic. Take a look at my five-generation chart at this point and you will see why. There is still a possibility that I might locate the marriage license of Louis Kruse and Lena Bernhard here in the United States. Even if this does happen I will still be two marriage licenses away from having accomplished my goal of locating all sixteen of my great-great-grandparents. In addition to the marriage license of Louis and Lena Kruse I would still need two more. One would be the marriage license of Hirsh Margolin and Temma Kranz and the other would be the marriage license of Matthias Wild and Maria Keller, which would provide the names of Maria's parents. If these last two documents exist they will be found on the other side of the ocean.

Leslie and I stay in touch and are always hoping that we will eventually be able to get together. So far, conflicting schedules have prevented this from happening. Leslie is a child psychologist who loves her work and her family, which take up a good part of her time. She has several grandchildren who also make demands for their fair share of her time. We have at times discussed the possibility of visiting Russia in a few years and I really look forward to that.

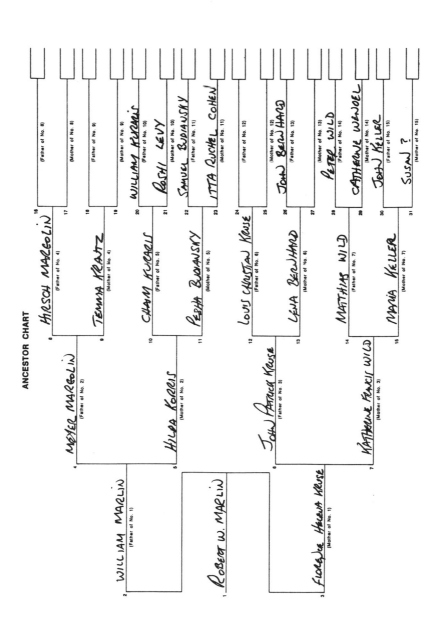

Ancestor chart—advanced.

Most of my time is taken up with numerous projects and pursuits related to genealogy. It is my firm belief that almost anyone can accomplish as much in their genealogical research as I have in mine, provided that they are willing to exert an equal amount of effort.

I leave with one final admonition, which is also the best piece of advice I can offer to anyone who wants to start a similar search. It is the bottom line of what I have repeatedly stated, and that is: Unless you are prepared to exert that extra effort and do the necessary homework, you are doomed to failure at worst and mediocrity at best. I personally hope you make the obvious choice. However you choose to do it, I sincerely wish you a lot of luck and hope you achieve as much satisfaction and happiness from doing your research as I have from mine.

CHAPTER 8

Primary Sources

The time has come to try to analyze and organize some of the data that has been presented. This is where an in-depth look at creative analysis begins. A few helpful suggestions are in order. First of all, remember the basic rule: There is no right or wrong way to proceed. Whatever works best for you is the only important thing. Second, I am not the ultimate authority on the best way for you to pursue this subject. There are dozens of possibilities that I haven't thought of yet, and I'm certain you will quickly discover many others on your own. Even after all this time, I still come up with new ways to improve my methods. Many of them are too mundane and time consuming for some, but they work for me and they might work for you. Third, when I say, "It is only important if you want to succeed," I am not being flippant or curt. I mean for those words to hit you hard. In research, going the "extra yard" can usually be translated into time, which is "going the extra hour." If you are familiar with Murphy's Law, you can bet that the most remote possibility is almost always the one that the geneal-ogist is looking for.

In the following pages I have listed what I consider the most important documents for you to work with. There are dozens of others that might be available, but these are the ones that most of our ancestors were forced to accept and live with. The items I have listed appear on many but not all documents. However, as I have consistently pointed out, each and every one of these documents has changed from year to year and from locality to locality. What I have included is only meant to serve as a basic guideline, designed to help you to develop your own creative analysis.

Vital Records: Birth, Marriage, and Death Records

Rich or poor, the law required the recording of birth, death, and marriage information. Although city directory records are somewhat hit and miss, they are still a valuable source. The ancestors of everyone in America came from somewhere else. It is only a matter of time and geography— how long ago and from where. Every one of these ancestors who came to America was also subjected to being recorded for many reasons other than vital records. Passenger arrival records and naturalization procedures are just two types of records that detail world history more accurately than most history books. The latest source of data is the Social Security death index. Almost anyone can make use of this source and it is fast growing in popularity for this reason. All of these documents fall into the category of what I call "primary records sources."

As I've stated, there are dozens of other types of records, but why bother with them until you have good reason to believe that a record for your family exists? If you are involved in genealogy as a hobby your time is probably limited. It is better to spend it dealing with those records that are most likely to produce the best results. To look through property rolls and probate records is, for the most part, a waste of time as a primary source. However, if a federal census indicates that your ancestor owned the house he was living in then it seems like a good idea to check property records right away. Generally speaking, however, it is a good idea to wait until after you have exhausted the other possibilities and found nothing to begin exploring these secondary sources.

When I found out that the Kruse family owned a grave site, I looked for and found a copy of the original deed. It provided no information but it was a nice piece of family memorabilia. Now, let's look at these primary sources and analyze their contents:

Birth Certificate

Name
Date of Birth
Place of Birth
Name of Father
Age of Father
Occupation of Father
Maiden Name of Mother
Age of Mother
Home Address of Family
Number of Children Born to This Woman
Number of Children Now Living

First and foremost, you must remember that the laws regarding the registration of births came into being in different parts of the country at different times and for different reasons. Even after the registration of births became mandatory many people simply ignored the law. Some people continued to have these events recorded only in church records. Others simply did nothing and the event went unrecorded. The family name given on a birth certificate is usually the family name of the father. If the mother was not married to the father, then the family name of the mother may be different.

This information was generally provided by the mother of the child, who may have wanted to provide a proper family name for her child and at the same time establish paternity. The spelling of the name on a birth certificate was sometimes the family's first attempt to Americanize the family name. Even though the family name may have been Bernhard, the birth certificate may record Bennett. This type of analysis is the most difficult. You almost have to get into the minds of your ancestors to try to figure out what they were thinking at that time.

Where the birth actually occurred may have some significance in regard to finding out what church the family belonged to. If the birth occurred in a Catholic hospital, it may indicate that the family was Catholic. If the birth occurred outside of the area where the family lived, it may simply indicate that the family may have been away from home for the day and the birth occurred unexpectedly. The father's name on a birth certificate can provide a number of clues as to whether or not the couple was married and whether or not they were living together at the time of the birth. In Christian families it is common for the first son to bear the name of the father. This creates the Senior and Junior titles. At times the child is the third in a line to bear the same name and becomes "John Jones III."

In Jewish families (and in many Italian families) the first male child is usually named after the paternal grandfather and the first female is named after the paternal grandmother.

Additional children were then named after the maternal grandparents. An exception occurred when a close, beloved relative, such as a brother or sister, passed away unexpectedly. Eastern European Jews generally do not name children after living relatives. However, the Sephardic or Mediterranean Jews do. Establishing who an ancestor is named after can help you in your search.

OTHER SOURCES

The birth certificates of the father and the mother are other sources. Simply subtract the age from the date on the child's birth certificate and search the birth index five years on each side of that year. Check old city directories around the year of this birth for the family at the address given on the birth certificate. Then check for others with the same surname who lived nearby. This could have been parents or brothers. The city directory may verify the father's occupation and might even supply the name of the business he owned or worked for. If you don't already know the maiden name of the mother, this opens a totally new avenue of research. For genealogical purposes the mother's family line should be just as important as the father's line. Knowing when this child was born should make it fairly easy to locate a marriage license. For example, if there had been three previous children, simply go back about five years and start searching the marriage index. If the count between the number of children born and the number still living indicates some difference, look up the death certificate for the deceased. It might lead to a family burial plot you don't know about. Also, send for copies of the birth certificates of the other siblings. You never know what might turn up. Look for patterns in the naming of the children. This might tell you the first names of other relatives you might not even be aware of.

Marriage License

Name of Groom
Home Address of Groom
Age of Groom
Birthplace of Groom
Occupation of Groom
Name of Bride
Home Address of Bride
Age of Bride
Birthplace of Bride
Name of Father of Groom
Maiden Name of Mother of Groom
Name of Father of Bride
Maiden Name of Mother of Bride
Address Where Ceremony Was Performed
Name and Address of Person Performing Ceremony
Names and Addresses of Witnesses
Signatures of Bride, Groom, and Witnesses

Normally, the marriage license provides the most information of the vital records group. If the certificate is for your parents, then you are automatically already back to the third generation of your genealogical chart. If you can locate the marriage license of either set of your grandparents you are indeed fortunate.

As with birth certificates, it is important to remember that a hundred years ago many people did not bother with civil documents. To my knowledge no accurate statistics exist indicating the percentage of people who were married by a religious ceremony, totally ignoring civil protocol. I have spent considerable time examining New York City indexes for the years 1890 to 1900. It surprises me to find that very few obviously Jewish names appeared during that period. After 1900 I have been able to locate almost anyone I have looked for. It is only speculation, but I believe that there is a reason for this. The second great wave of Jewish immigration began about 1888 and continued well into the second decade of the 1900s. The first group of the wave of 1888 to 1898 were simply ignorant of civil laws and therefore continued to use the time-honored rites of Judaism to solemnize these occasions. Later on they realized the importance of civil registry of vital records, and slowly consented to following them. They still had the actual ceremony performed in the synagogue, but they also went through the civil paperwork routine.

When people intent on marrying realized that their children were citizens by virtue of their American birth, the civil record became especially important and apparent. The marriage license now became proof of the years lived in the United States for naturalization purposes. There were numerous other similar benefits to following civil protocol. I can speak with some authority about this with regard to Jews, because these facts have been pointed out to me during discussions of this subject with several elderly Jews who either remembered them personally or had the information passed on to them. It is my belief that other ethnic groups went through a similar metamorphosis. Many early immigrants from various ethnic backgrounds were only married in Catholic and Protestant church ceremonies. However, when the value of civil records for citizenship or naturalization purposes became apparent their thinking also changed.

Many continued to get married in church, but also observed civil protocol.

The age given in a marriage license is the key to obtaining the birth certificates for both bride and groom. Some marriage licenses give the exact date of birth. If the bride or groom was born in the United States, obtaining a birth certificate for both should not be a problem. As stated earlier, this availability is set by local and state government agencies. If the bride and groom are foreign born, it may be necessary to do further research to determine the year of arrival in order to check arrival records.

Home addresses can be checked in city directories to find information regarding other possible family members listed, occupations, or perhaps where the family members were employed. This might include the brothers or sisters of the bride and groom. At times when you can't locate records for your direct-line relatives, you can trace them through one of their brothers or sisters.

The names of both sets of parents can sometimes lead to their marriage license. For example, suppose the groom was twenty-one when he was married, and was born in the United States. The possibility then exists that his parents may have been married in America. Check the marriage index starting with the groom's birth year. Also check the city directories for those years for families listed under the maiden name of the mother. She may even be listed there as living at home with her parents before marriage. This avenue of research has endless possibilities. Where the ceremony was performed and the address might possibly tell you that the couple were married in a church and where that church was located. Even if the church no longer exists it might be possible to find additional records by locating the archives where the church records were deposited. The person performing the ceremony might be of some importance, especially if this person was a family member. The names of witnesses can always open up new avenues to explore. Most of the time they were very close friends or even family members. Having signatures on hand to compare with earlier documents is always helpful. All in all, the marriage license has some of the best and most helpful information available for the genealogist.

Death Certificate

Date of Death	Where Death Occurred
Home Address	Name of Spouse
Marital Status	Age in Years, Months, and Days
Date of Birth	Industry
Occupation	Years in the United States
Birthplace	Birthplace of Father
Name of Father	Birthplace of Mother
Maiden Name of Mother	Relationship to Deceased
Informant	Location
Cemetery	
Name and Address of Undertaker	
Name and Address of Physician	
Cause of Death and Length of Illness	

The death certificate generally has the least number of restrictions on its availability and, therefore, is the easiest document of the vital records group to obtain. In some states the death certificate is a public record with no restrictions. I have been able to obtain death certificates for people who have died as late as 1990, by simply stating that the document was to be used for "family genealogical research." Like all other vital records, the availability is different from state to state, as well as county to county and city to city. Even when a restriction is in force it may not apply to direct-line or other close family members. Don't be afraid to make a request. The worst that can happen is that your request may be denied.

The death certificate is in some ways the least accurate of the vital records. In other ways, it is the most accurate. As pointed out earlier, the information it contains is not supplied by the person who possessed the most accurate information about the deceased. Of course, I am referring to the deceased themselves. In many cases this information is not even supplied by the person closest to them. Mothers and fathers may be close to hysteria. The wife may be too distraught to even talk.

The role of informant usually fell on the oldest, calmest close relative available. That person may have only been guessing about the most important details. In many cases, the age given is an approximate figure, give or take five or six years. The number of years in America is also usually provided in round numbers. Answers such as, "He got here about sixty years ago," or "About as long as I'm here, which is about forty years," was an acceptable answer. The doctor who was recording this information was only interested in completing his duty by filling in as much information as possible.

In many cases the names and birthplaces of the parents of the deceased had long been forgotten. In most cases the maiden name of the mother was not known, even to her children. Also, remember that the celebration of a birthday is a relatively new American custom. It was just another day to many early immigrants, and many simply did not know the month and day of their birth. This information is included in other official documents and will be covered soon.

The main thing to remember is that even though some of the information in the death certificate is approximate or simply an educated guess, it is certainly a place to begin your research. Even if the figure indicating the number of years in the United States is off by ten years, it has still narrowed down your search. All in all, the range of information in a death certificate can open up many other avenues for you to pursue and to gather additional information.

<h2>OTHER SOURCES</h2>

If the deceased was born in the United States the first thing to look for is a birth certificate. Knowing where the death occurred and the home address of the deceased are the first leads in researching city directories in the manner previously described. If the deceased was a widow or widower, look for information on the spouse. Some death certificates will supply the given name of the spouse, even when they are deceased. The date or year of birth can lead you to many sources other than the birth certificate. If it occurred around the turn of the century in America, the federal censuses are a good place to start.

The occupation and industry, once again, can be found in many death certificates. It has not been mentioned before, but in the absence of death certificates in the geographical area you are researching, you might try using the telephone directory. However, my personal experience with phone directories has convinced me that they are a source of last resort for genealogical purposes. That is the reason I have not mentioned it until now. It will be discussed under the heading of city directories.

The length of time in America can easily lead to obtaining the Declaration of Intention, Petition for Naturalization, and passenger arrival records. Even though you may not know the exact year, the number of years to be searched will have been cut down considerably. The names of parents and their birthplaces were discussed under birth certificates. Once again, if they are foreign born, be sure to check all documentation pertaining to arrival and naturalization. If they were here in America early in this century, then turn to federal census schedules.

All death certificates do not name the informant. When they do, I have found this to be an invaluable source of information. In some cases I found that the informant was still living at the same address shown on the death certificate even though twenty to thirty years had elapsed. Getting in touch with them sometimes required little more than a letter of inquiry. I have found that a short, well-written note will produce better results than a telephone call. It gives the person time to think about their response and allows them to answer at their own convenience. Uninvited and unexpected phone calls may produce a bad reaction that you can ill afford to chance.

Anyone who has done genealogical research in cemeteries can appreciate the importance of them as a source. Cemetery authorities can be a lot of help should you want to contact living family members. A short note explaining why you want to contact the family is all that is necessary. Sometimes the cemetery is already in touch with family members who pay annually for grave site maintenance. Other times they will simply supply you with the last known address of the next of kin shown on their records. In most cases they are not legally required to respond to your inquiry. Therefore it is not a bad idea to enclose a check for $10 to cover the cost of their time and effort. They are a business and entitled to be compensated for services of this type when rendered. This never applies to government agencies who usually charge for the services they supply.

When visiting a cemetery you never know what you might find. In addition to information about the deceased, you sometimes discover an entire family. In the case of Jewish people, this bonus is extended. For example, almost all Jewish headstones contain more than just the name of the deceased. They also contain the name of the father of the deceased. Sometimes the headstone also includes other family information. The information found in cemeteries is unique in each case and almost always makes the trip worthwhile.

Knowing the name of the undertaker can also sometimes put you in touch with living family members. This has worked for me on several occasions when the obituary mentioned the name of the funeral home. I simply wrote a short note explaining why I was trying to contact the family and they simply passed the note on to the family, who in turn contacted me.

The name of the attending physician and the type and length of illness have become extremely important. The science of genetics has come of age. It is important to have some knowledge about the medical history of your family in order to aid your doctor in the event someone in your family becomes ill. It has been discovered with certainty that many of the genetically transmitted illnesses and diseases, which in the past have affected earlier family members, are now a possible threat to your children and grandchildren. If your research shows that a number of family members died from the same disease, it is not a bad idea to let other family members know so that they can have their family checked for possible symptoms of that disease or illness.

City Directories

Name
Home Address
Name of Business
Business Address
Occupation
Name of Spouse
Name of Children Living at Home
Occupation of Children

In my opinion, the city directory is consistently the most neglected source of genealogical information available. I have spoken with people involved in genealogical research for years who have never even heard of them. I began using them starting with the 1850 New York City directories when I was looking for the Kruse and Bernhard families. I also used them when tracing the Wild family in Boston from 1874 to 1888, and again when looking for the Margolin and Korris families between 1900 and 1910. For example, my grandmother's brother, Meyer Korris, had moved to Buffalo, New York, sometime around 1914. His father, Hyman, was then living with him. However, I had already established that Hyman was living with Hilda and Meyer Margolin when the 1920 census was conducted. Would this be reflected in the city directory? Take a look. It shows Hyman and Meyer at the same address in the 1920 Buffalo City directory. Nineteen twenty-one is the last year for which Hyman is listed, and it appears that he must have thereafter left town. As you can see, the various entries include the business name and address. The name Korris & Herring had some family significance. I was already aware that Meyer was married to a lady whose maiden name was Sarah Herring and that Nathan was his brother-in-law. At the time this research was done, it was not necessary to go any farther.

The only alternative to the city directory is the telephone directory, more commonly known as the T/D. To my knowledge, very few old telephone directories exist from earlier than the mid-1920s, because most people could not afford a telephone. Thus they only contained listings of people who were affluent enough to afford a telephone. The telephone did not become an everyday, every-home item until the mid-1930s. During World War II, telephone installation was done on a priority basis. In the area I grew up in during this period, Brooklyn, New York, only two families on our street had telephones. Inasmuch as more than seventy families lived on this street, this was certainly a tiny percentage. By 1946 most everyone had a telephone. This is part of the reason I do not consider telephone directories a true source for genealogical research. At best they are secondary. Without belaboring the point, all I can add is that I much prefer using city directories whenever they are available.

OTHER SOURCES

Using again the Korris family as an example, after locating them in the 1920 city directory the first thing would be to look for additional entries for Gertrude, or for any other children of Meyer Korris who might appear at a later date. Gertrude was listed in the city directories for the first time in 1950. This would make her about eighteen, which in turn makes her birth year about 1932. In this case, if the people listed in the city directories are direct-line relatives, a request for the 1930 and 1940 census schedules might be in order. Remember that it will be necessary for you to supply a death certificate in order to obtain this information.

Koronowski Isadore grocer 1708 Clinton
" Ludwig r 1708 Clinton
Koropecaki Metro lab r 214 Miami
Korowsky Nathan carp r 14 Bristol
Korpul John lab r 81 Lanx
Korpuss John lab r 23 Cambria
Korrey Elias mach r 356 Swan
Korris Meyer peddler r 157 Monroe
Korsak Anthony lab r 19 Rother ave
Korsby Charles mech r 5 Oak
Korsielowski Martin lab r 805 S Division

1919

Korowsky Nathan peddler r 14 Bristol
Korpan Anthony molder r 402 Hertel ave
Korpus John foundryman r 542 Willet
Korrey Abdo lab r 356 Swan
Korris Hyman r 157 Monroe
" Meyer (Korris & Herring) r 157 Mon-
   roe
" & Herring (Meyer Korris and Meyer
   Herring) woolens 235 William
Korst Arthur r 440 Prospect ave
" Arthur (Korst Summer & Szabo) r 997
   Fillmore ave
" Elizabeth wid Jacob r 821 Woodlawn
" Ernestino china decorator r 89 Wasmuth

1920

Korona Jacob harness mkr r 11 Concord
" Peter mach r 364 Wilson
Koronowski Chester mach r 791 Sycamore
" Isadore mach r 30 Stanislaus
Korris Hyman r 157 Monroe
" Meyer (Korris & Herring) r 157 Monroe
" & Herring (Meyer Korris and Meyer
   Herring) woolens 235 William
Korst Arthur (Szabo Korst & Wirth) r 985
   Genesee
" Elizabeth wid Jacob r 821 Woodlawn

1921

Korpan Antony mldr h402 Hertel av
Korporaal John pntr r988 Elk
Korris Meyer (Korris Woolen Co) 139 William h
   do
" Woolen Co (Meyer Korris) 139 William
Korry Fannie Mrs h146 Emslie
Korsie Albert dept mgr Gerber Nott & Co r167
   Best
Korsock Anthony lab h59 Beck

1925

" John r69 Clayton
" Paul lab r60 Clayton
Korpanty Chas B (Julia) tailer h241 Swan av
Korsonics James lab r178 N Division
Korris Meyer (Sarah) tailor 161 (81) William h do
Kuffman (Ben) cigars 404 Clinton h120
   Hertel av
Korat Frank (Mary) shoe repr 132 Hamilton h55
   Thompson
Korst Arth (Anna; Theatre Hotel) h47 E Mohawk

1930

" Anthony (Anna) lab Fetter Steel Barrel Corp h406
   Hertel av
" Simon r406 Hertel av
Korpanty Chas (Virginia) buttonhole clk h469 Koons av
Korsons Mitchell lab r178 North Division
Korris Meyer (Sarah) 2d hd clothing 165 William h do

Korris Alex J earn r08 Thompson
" Frank (Mary) shoe repr 119 Thompson h do
Korsnylowski Walter lab r370 Germania

1935

" Steven engy hw News r498 Hertel av
Korpanty Chas S (Virginia) tailer h52 Crosman
" Karol S (Julia) tailer 119 Walden av h469 Koons
" Matthew announcer Polish Broadcasting Bureau r64
   Franklin
Korpar Peter pntr r70 Richmond av
Korris Meyer 2d hd clo 165 William h do
" Jennie S slswn S S Kresge Co r99 Thompson
" Theo (Mary) slsse repr 99 Thompson h do
Korst Raymond C (Ernestine) pntr Hecker Products
   Corp h89 Wasmuth av

1940

" Chas S jr mech r52 Crosman
" Julia M (wid Karl) h106 Gibson
" Matthew (Irene) announcer Polish Broadcasting Bureau
   r Cheektowaga NY
Korris Gertrude student r17 Hamlin rd
" Meyer (Sarah) h17 Hamlin rd

" Dorothy ofc wkr card Chevrolet Div h144 Thompson
" Dorothy clk Merch Mut Casualty r99 Thompson
" Marion slswn Goode Cake Shops r99 Thompson
" Theo (Mary) mldr h99 Thompson

1950

Korowesis Gust (Helen) clo chsr 829 Main h87 Riley
" Kay clk r87 Riley
Korpanty Chas (Betty) assmblr Chevrolet h20 Hurlock av
" Julia M (wid Karl) h106 Gibson
" Virginia (wid Chas) tailer h52 Crosman
Korris Meyer (Sarah) h17 Hamlin rd
Korth Alex (Mary) tchr PS h144 Thompson
" Dorothy ofc wkr Westinghouse r99 Thompson
" Marian opr NYTel r99 Thompson
" Theo (Mary) wtchman Lederer Term Whse h99 Thomp-
   son
Korshylowsky Walter contr r370 Germania
Korst Anita L ofc sec r245 Kingsley
" Raymond C (Ernestine L) h89 Wasmuth av
" Wm (Clare) mech Am Optical Co h245 Kingsley
Korszlowski Leo r818 South Division
" Martin (Martha) Jan h818 South Division
" Mary F sten Cargill Inc r Hamburg

1952

Korpanty Chas (Betty) assmblr Chev Mtr h20 Hurlock av
" Julia M (wid Karl) h106 Gibson
" Matt (Irene) dir Polonia Varieties Program r Cheektowaga
" Richd ship clk Libbey-Owens r52 Crosman
" Virginia (wid Chas) tailer h52 Crosman
Korpilewicz Walter Rev asst pastor St Stanislaus RC
   Church r123 Townsend
Korris Meyer (Sarah) h17 Hamlin rd
Korth Alex (Marg) tchr PS h144 Thompson
" Dorothy ofcwkr Westinghouse r99 Thompson
" Theo (Mary) wtchman h99 Thompson
Korshylowsky Walter contr r370 Germania
Korst Donald r232 Elmwood av

1955

" Richd A drftsmn US Eng r52 Crosman av
" Virginia (wid Chas) tailer h52 Crosman av
Korpilewicz Walter Rev asst pastor St Stanislaus RC
   Ch r123 Townsend
Korris Meyer (Sarah) h17 Hamlin rd
Korth Alex (Marg) tchr PS h144 Thompson
" Mary (wid Theo) h99 Thompson
Korshylowsky Walter contr r370 Germania
Korsinski Wm (Arlene) grndr Bliss-Loughlin h1895 Clin-
   ton
Korst Raymond C (Ernestine L) h89 Wasmuth av
" Wm (Clare) mech Am Optical Co h245 Kingsley
Korszylowski Leo lab Simon Bros r818 South Division
" Martin (Martha) jan Bflo Optical r818 South Division

1956

" Richd A eng drftsma US Eng r52 Crosman av
" Virginia (wid Chas) h52 Crosman av
Korpar Peter r361 Pennsylvania
Korpilewicz Walter Rev asst pastor St Stanislaus RC
   Ch r123 Townsend
Korpnick Kenneth bonder Wagner Electric r44 Lester
Korris Meyer (Sarah) h17 Hamlin rd
Korth Alex (Marg) tchr PS h144 Thompson
" Mary (wid Theo) h99 Thompson
Korshylowsky Walter contr Bflo Slag r370 Germania
Korris Sue Ann sten & clk Franklin-Cowan Paper Co
   Inc r22 Olympic
Korst John H corres U S Gypsum r Hamburg NY

1957

Buffalo City Directory 1920 to 1957 listing the family of Meyer Korris.

The city directories most popular with genealogists cover the years 1850 to 1933. For that period almost all related censuses are available for cross-reference. The notable exception is the 1930 federal census, which has not yet been opened. Noting the first year someone was listed in the city directory might indicate that he had immigrated within the last couple of years before that. If the years in which you located your ancestor were before 1900, it might be fruitful to check the pre-1906 naturalization records. If a city directory shows children living at home, count back about eighteen years and look through the birth index. There are dozens of uses for the information found in the city directories.

Declaration of Intention
(To Become Citizen)

Court Where the Declaration Was Filed
Age
Date of Birth
Occupation
Present Residence
Physical Description
Overseas Port Immigrated From
Name of Ship
Arrival Date
Port of Entry
Date D.O.I. Was Filed
Court Where Declaration Was Filed

The Declaration of Intention has been around for a long time. Prior to 1906, this document contained little more than the name and address of the person who filed it. This initial "first paper" could be filed in any court in America. In turn, the Petition for Naturalization could also be filed in any court, simply by producing a court-certified copy of the Declaration of Intention.

After 1906, naturalization became a "federally" supervised procedure, although it could still be carried out in nonfederal courts. However, after 1906 all forms and documentation became standardized. It also became mandatory for courts to file copies of all documents with the U.S. Department of Immigration & Naturalization Service.

As you can see on the post-1906 Declaration of Intention for Abraham Korris, this document is quite detailed. However, as already stated it still was not mandatory for the petitioner to file his Petition for Naturalization in the same court as the Declaration of Intention was filed in. It was not even necessary to file it in the same state.

My grandmother's brother, Abe Korris, is a classic example. As you can see, his Declaration of Intention was filed in Brooklyn, New York. However, his Petition for Naturalization was filed on September 24, 1913, in New Jersey.

This document can be your first link to the world your ancestor left behind. It can be a paperwork bridge across an ocean. The samples shown actually tell you all you need to know to cross that bridge. However, this particular Declaration of Intention was filed after 1906. The Declaration of Intention before that time may, or may not, have included any or all of this information. The rule of thumb seems to be that the earlier these documents were filed, the less information they contain. The very fact that a Declaration of Intention is filed indicates not only that the person was not born in the United States, but also that he or she was most likely a newcomer to America. This description applies mainly to post-1906 Declarations of Intention, because they theoretically became standardized after that year and therefore theoretically contain the same data. Pre-1906 Declarations of Inten-

No. 5622   Form 2203   TRIPLICATE
[To be given to the person making the Declaration]

UNITED STATES OF AMERICA

Department of Commerce and Labor
BUREAU OF IMMIGRATION AND NATURALIZATION
DIVISION OF NATURALIZATION

DECLARATION OF INTENTION
(Invalid for all purposes seven years after the date hereof)

STATE OF NEW YORK,
COUNTY OF KINGS. } ss: In the SUPREME   Court
of   NEW YORK.

3. *Abraham Korriss*, aged *23* years;
occupation *Laborer*, do declare on oath/affirm that my personal
description is: Color *White*, complexion *Fair*, height *5* feet *9* inches,
weight *155* pounds, color of hair *Black*, color of eyes *Brown*,
other visible distinctive marks *none*
; I was born in *Kieff, Russia*
, on the *28"* day of *July*, anno
Domini 1*885*; I now reside at *361 South 3" Street*
I emigrated to the United States of America from *Antwerp, Belgium*
on the vessel *Norland* [If the alien arrived otherwise than by vessel, the character of conveyance or name of transportation company should be given.]; my last
foreign residence was *Kieff, Russia*
It is my bona fide intention to renounce forever all allegiance and fidelity to any foreign
prince, potentate, state, or sovereignty, and particularly to
_____, of which I am now a citizen/subject; I
arrived at the port of *New York*, in the
State
Territory of *New York* on or about the *22"* day
District
of *May*, anno Domini 1*906*; I am not an anarchist; I am not a
polygamist nor a believer in the practice of polygamy; and it is my intention in good faith
to become a citizen of the United States of America and to permanently reside therein:
SO HELP ME GOD.

Abraham Korris
(Original signature of declarant.)

Subscribed and sworn to/affirmed before me this *9"*

[SEAL.]   day of *December*, anno Domini 19*08*

Frank Ehlers,
Clerk of the SUPREME   Court.
By *_____* Deputy Clerk.

Declaration of Intention of Abraham Korris.

№ 6475

17

U.S. DEPARTMENT OF LABOR
NATURALIZATION SERVICE

ORIGINAL

UNITED STATES OF AMERICA

PETITION FOR NATURALIZATION

CLERK'S OFFICE
SEP 24 1913

To the Honorable the Court of Common Pleas in and for Hudson County, New Jersey:

The petition of _Abraham Korris_, hereby filed, respectfully shows:

First. My place of residence is _346 Berguline Av. Town of Union_, New Jersey.

Second. My occupation is _Merchant_.

Third. I was born on the _18_ day of _July_, anno Domini _1885_ at _Russia_.

Fourth. I emigrated to the United States from _Antwerp, Belgium_ on or about the _7_ day of _May_, anno Domini _1906_, and arrived in the United States, at the port of _New York_ on the _22_ day of _May_ anno Domini _1906_ on the vessel _Vaderland_.

Fifth. I declared my intention to become a citizen of the United States on the _14_ day of _Dec_, anno Domini _191?_ at _Brooklyn N.Y._ in the _Supreme_ Court of _Kings County_.

Sixth. I am married. My wife's name is _Nettie_, she was born at _Ashliew Russia_ and now resides at _346 Berguline Av. Town of Union_.

I have _one_ children, and the name, date and place of birth, and place of residence of each of said children is as follows:

Pohin N.Y. Feb 1913 Town of Union 346 Berguline Av. Union

Seventh. I am not a disbeliever in or opposed to organized government or a member of or affiliated with any organization or body of persons teaching disbelief in or opposition to organized government. I am not a polygamist nor a believer in the practice of polygamy. I am attached to the principles of the Constitution of the United States, and it is my intention to become a citizen of the United States and to renounce absolutely and forever all allegiance and fidelity to any foreign prince, potentate, state, or sovereignty, and particularly to NICHOLAS II. EMPEROR OF ALL THE RUSSIAS of whom at this time I am a subject, and it is my intention to reside permanently in the United States.

Eighth. I am able to speak the English language.

Ninth. I have resided continuously in the United States of America for the term of five years at least, immediately preceding the date of this petition, to wit, since the _22_ day of _May_, anno Domini _1906_ and in the State of New Jersey, continuously next preceding the date of this petition, since the _28_ day of _Aug_, anno Domini _1910_, being a residence within this State of at least one year next preceding the date of this petition.

Tenth. I have not heretofore made petition for citizenship to any court. (I made petition for citizenship to the _____ Court at _____ in the _____ day of _____ anno Domini _____ and such petition was denied by the said COURT for the following reasons and causes, to wit: _____ and the cause of such denial has since been cured or removed.)

Attached hereto and made a part of this petition are my declaration of intention to become a citizen of the United States and the certificate from the Department of Labor, together with my affidavit and the affidavits of the two verifying witnesses thereto, required by law. Wherefore your petitioner prays that he may be admitted a citizen of the United States of America.

Abraham Korris
(Complete and true signature of petitioner.)

Declaration of Intention and Certificate of Arrival No. _____ from Department of Labor filed this _____ day of _Apt._ 191 3.

AFFIDAVITS OF PETITIONER AND WITNESSES.

STATE OF NEW JERSEY,
County of Hudson.

The aforesaid petitioner being duly sworn, deposes and says that he is the petitioner in the above-entitled proceedings; that he has read the foregoing petition and knows the contents thereof; that the said petition is signed with his full, true name; that the same is true of his own knowledge except as to matters therein stated to be alleged upon information and belief, and that as to those matters he believes it to be true.

Abraham Korris
(Complete and true signature of petitioner.)

Elias Singer, occupation _Lawyer_, residing at _744 Berguline ..._, and _Meyer Korris_, occupation _Merchant_, residing at _346_, each being severally, duly, and respectively sworn, deposes and says that he is a citizen of the United States of America; that he has personally known _Abraham Korris_, the petitioner above mentioned, to have resided in the United States continuously immediately preceding the date of filing his petition, since the _25_ day of _Sept._, anno Domini _1907_ and in the State in which the above-entitled petition is made continuously since the _28_ day of _July_, anno Domini _1910_; and that he has personal knowledge that the said petitioner is a person of good moral character, attached to the principles of the Constitution of the United States, and that the petitioner is in every way qualified, in his opinion, to be admitted a citizen of the United States.

Elias Singer

Petition for Naturalization of Abraham Korris.

tion may or may not contain any or all of the same information.

The Declaration of Intention is the only document I know of that gives any detailed information regarding the person's physical description. The primary reason this information was included was to prevent anyone from stealing this document and then being able to use it to obtain citizenship. It also prevented the sale of this document to a known criminal who had already been denied citizenship. In many cases it not only tells you the name of the country in which the person was born, but also the city or village.

If you wish to learn more about the historical path your ancestor followed after coming to America and filing his declaration, then the information it contains can be used to locate other documents such as census records, death and birth records, and other information that might tell you when their children arrived, their residence movements, and their various occupations.

However, if you are ready to cross that ocean bridge the Declaration of Intention is your bridge. There are four pieces of information on it that are invaluable to your research. The three most important notations are the name of the ship the person arrived on, the date the ship arrived, and the port of arrival. The fourth important note is the port the person left from. With this information, it is now possible to go directly to the passenger arrival records and check the manifest of the vessel that the person arrived on. More on passenger lists coming up.

Pre-1906 Naturalization Records

Name
Home Address
Occupation
Birth Date or Age
Former Nationality
Port of Arrival in United States
Date of Arrival
Name of Witness

Address of Witness
Date of Naturalization
Court of Naturalization

As you can see, the pre-1906 naturalization records, at their best, usually have less than a dozen pieces of information of use to genealogists. I say "at their best," because the items listed above are a list of the blank boxes that appear on pre-1906 index cards. The format for these index cards did not come into existence until sometime in the 1930s when these records were indexed.

This format was designed to cover all of the items that appeared on most of the later naturalizations, which took place from about 1840 to 1906. If you look at the samples included, you can see that the earlier naturalization contained virtually no detailed information. Therefore many of the boxes were left blank. As time passed and the court systems handling these proceedings became a little more sophisticated, they also demanded more information. By the turn of the century many of the items listed had become standard questions in all courts, which in turn meant less blank spaces on these index cards.

However, all of these proceedings were not totally standardized until after 1906. Therefore, how much information you find will still vary greatly depending upon the location where the naturalization proceeding took place. It is interesting to note that there were very few females submitting applications for naturalization. This is because our society at that time was totally male dominated. Women usually became citizens when they married. Very few women applied for citizenship through the naturalization process.

Like the Declaration of Intention, this document is a direct link between where the person is now and where they came from. After 1906, "these naturalization papers" came in two parts, although their ultimate function was still to prove citizenship. After 1906, a Petition for Naturalization was filed a few years after the Declaration of Intention. When the petition was granted a certificate was issued, which conferred citizenship. The certificate contained little information other than the name of the petitioner.

In pre-1906 naturalizations, the Declaration of Intention is usually more valuable because it includes the date of arrival in the United States, as well as the name of the ship. In any case, both of these documents represent a paperwork bridge across the ocean. As stated earlier, you may never run across the Declaration of Intention because it may have originally been filed in a different court and may be buried in those court records forever. If that is the case, the naturalization papers usually serve the same purpose. If you wish to learn more about a person and his family from a historical standpoint, then the sources to check should be obvious by now.

However, if you want to start at the place of origin and ancestral roots of your ancestors, then this document will help get you there. If it contains the date of arrival and the port of arrival, it is a matter of checking all passenger arrival manifests for that date. This might mean checking through the manifests of eight or nine ships for any given day. But this is not an insurmountable task. It should not take more than a few hours to accomplish. Comments on passenger lists will follow a description of post-1906 naturalization proceedings.

Post-1906 Naturalization Documents

Name
Address
Occupation
Place of Birth
Date of Birth
Date of D.O.I.
Court of D.O.I.
Name of Spouse
Date of Birth of Spouse
Date of Death If Deceased
When Spouse Entered U.S.
Name of Last Foreign Residence
Name of Port Immigrated From
Name Used When Entering United States
Date of Entry and Name of Ship
Physical Description of Applicant
Names and Birth Dates of All Children
Names and Addresses of Two Witnesses
Signature of Petitioner
Signature of Both Witnesses

What can I add? The amount of information shown above is a composite of the information contained in the Declara-

Declaration of Intention of Hilda Margolin.

tion of Intention and Petition for Naturalization. Most of the information in the Declaration of Intention is repeated. There are two notable exceptions. The first is the physical description, while the second is a photograph of the applicant. This made it far more difficult, if not impossible, for anyone to use the Declaration of Intention of another person.

ORIGINAL
(To be retained by clerk)

UNITED STATES OF AMERICA

SS

PETITION FOR NATURALIZATION   No. 279933

2. District   Court of   Eastern District   at   Brooklyn, N.Y.

To the Honorable the _____ 2. District _____ Court of _____ Eastern District _____ at _____

The petition of _____ HILDA MARGOLIN _____ hereby filed, respectfully shows:

(1) My place of residence is _____ 399 Troy Ave. Bklyn. NY _____ (2) My occupation is Housewife

(3) I was born in _____ Korsin Kliev, Russia _____ on Dec. 15, 1878 _____ My race is Hebrew

(4) I declared my intention to become a citizen of the United States on Apr. 29, 1937 _____ in the Eastern District

Court of _____ United States _____ at _____ Brooklyn, NY

(5) I am _____ widow _____. The name of my wife or husband is was Meyer

we were married on Feb. 1903 _____ at New York, NY _____ ; he was born at Minsk, Russia

on Sept. 18, 1868 _____ entered the United States at New York, NY _____ on 1893 _____ for permanent residence therein,

and now resides at _____ deceased Dec. 1938 in Bklyn. NY _____ naturalized on _____

at _____ certificate No. _____ I have 5 _____ children, and the name, date,

and place of birth, and place of residence of each of said children are as follows: Samuel-Jan. 22, 1905-Russia-Bklyn

Paul-May 8, 1908-Bklyn-Maspeth, LI

William-Feb. 16, 1910-Bklyn-Bklyn

Ruth-Jan. 22, 1915-Bklyn-Bklyn

Theodore-Apr. 3, 1921-Bklyn-Bklyn

(6) My last foreign residence was _____ Boslov, Russia _____ I emigrated to the United States of

America from _____ Hamburg, Germany _____ My lawful entry for permanent residence in the United States

was at _____ New York, NY _____, under the name of _____ Hilda Korris

_____ 1893 _____, on the vessel _____ unknown

(7) I am not a disbeliever in or opposed to organized government or a member of or affiliated with any organization or body of persons teaching disbelief in or opposed to organized government. I am not a polygamist nor a believer in the practice of polygamy. I am attached to the principles of the Constitution of the United States and well disposed to the good order and happiness of the United States. It is my intention to become a citizen of the United States and to renounce absolutely and forever all allegiance and fidelity to any foreign prince, potentate, state, or sovereignty, of whom (which) at this time I am a subject (or citizen), and it is my intention to reside permanently in the United States. (8) I am able to speak the English language. (9) I have resided continuously in the United States of America for the term

of 5 years at least immediately preceding the date of this petition, to wit, since _____ 1893

and in the County of _____ Kings _____ this State, continuously next preceding the date of this petition, since

_____ 1893 _____ being a residence within said county of at least 6 months next preceding the date of this petition.

(10) I have _____ not _____ heretofore made petition for naturalization: No. _____ on _____

at _____ and such petition was denied by that Court for the following reasons and causes, to wit:

and the cause of such denial has since been cured or removed.

Attached hereto and made a part of this, my petition for naturalization, are my declaration of intention to become a citizen of the United States, and the affidavits of the two verifying witnesses required by law.

Wherefore, I, your petitioner, pray that I may be admitted a citizen of the United States of America, and that my name be changed to _____

I, _____ HILDA MARGOLIN _____ do swear (affirm) that I know the contents of this petition for naturalization subscribed by me, that the same is true to the best of my own knowledge, except as to matters therein stated to be alleged upon information and belief, and that as to those matters I believe them to be true, and that this petition was signed by me with my full, true name: SO HELP ME GOD.

Hilda Margolin

AFFIDAVITS OF WITNESSES

Bella Sachar _____ occupation Housewife & Saleslady

residing at _____ 611 Nostrand Ave. Bklyn, NY _____, and

Samuel L. Budinoff _____ occupation Retired

residing at _____ 865 Montgomery St. Bklyn, NY _____

each being severally, duly, and respectively sworn, deposes and says: I am a citizen of the United States of America; I have personally known and have been acquainted

in the United States with _____ HILDA MARGOLIN _____ the petitioner above mentioned,

since _____ Jan. 1, 1934 _____ and that to my personal knowledge the petitioner has resided in the United States continuously preceding

the date of filing this petition, of which this affidavit is a part, to wit, since the date last mentioned and at _____ Brooklyn, NY

in the County of _____ Kings

this State, in which the above-entitled petition is made, continuously since _____ Jan. 1, 1934 _____ and that I have personal knowledge that the petitioner has and during all such periods has been a person of good moral character, attached to the principles of the Constitution of the United States, and well disposed to the good order and happiness of the United States, and in my opinion the petitioner is in every way qualified to be admitted a citizen of the United States. I do swear (affirm) that the statements of fact I have made in this petition for naturalization subscribed by me are true to the best of my knowledge and belief.

Bella Sachar   *Samuel L. Budinoff*

Subscribed and sworn to before me by the above-named petitioner and witnesses in the respective forms of oath shown above in the office of Clerk of said Court at

Brooklyn, NY, this 2 day of May Anno Domini 19 40 _____

_____, showing the lawful entry for permanent residence of the petitioner above named, together with Declaration of Intention No. _____

of such petitioner, has been by me filed with, attached to, and made a part of this petition on this date.

Petition for Naturalization of Hilda Margolin

OTHER SOURCES

With perhaps one exception, most other leads should be obvious by this time. If these documents were to turn up in a box of old family papers they would certainly be a real bonanza of information. They should automatically lead you to numerous other documents such as birth, marriage, and death records, as well as almost every other source we have already discussed except passenger arrival records, which are the next topic of discussion. The names and addresses of the two witnesses in the petition can also be an extremely valuable clue. In this case, Bella Sachar is the sister of my grandmother Hilda. Samuel L. Budinoff was their first cousin. Most of the time, petitioners used close relatives as character witnesses. Therefore, the witnesses in your documents may be additional relatives you are not aware of.

Immigrant and Passenger Arrival Records

The above title is from the cover of a catalog by the same name issued by the National Archives. Most of the microfilm listed in this catalog covers the period between 1820 and 1954. Although many researchers refer to this material as "passenger arrival records," this is a misnomer. Some of this film is actually United States Customs Passenger Lists, and other parts of it are Immigration and Naturalization Service Lists. The catalog covers most Eastern Seaboard ports of arrival, as well as some Gulf of Mexico ports as far west as New Orleans. Because of the complexity of this material, I would not even attempt to go into any detail regarding the history of shipping, or how and why passenger lists were kept. Instead, I will try to explain what I consider the best way to attempt to find people who are on these lists. Let me just add that there are all sorts of irregular patterns that appear when using this source.

For example, there are occasions when a passenger manifest and an immigration list will appear on the same roll, one behind the other. This fact was discovered accidentally when I checked the passenger arrival manifest of the S.S. *Pretoria*. Finding the entry for Harry Margolin only took five minutes. However, the film was so light that it was impossible to make a photocopy. Even at maximum setting, all the machine produced was a blank sheet. In sheer frustration I started to rewind the film. After several quick turns I realized that I was going in the wrong direction. As I started to reverse, my eyes zeroed in on the name Margolin. Inasmuch as I had just left that entry, my first thought was that I had done something to the film. A closer inspection showed that I had accidentally stopped on the name Harry Margolin again. However, this time I was not looking at the passenger manifest. I was looking at another list. It turned out to be an immigration list for the same ship. This additional list included information that was not included in the passenger manifest. This was something I hadn't run into before. A passenger manifest and an immigration list, one behind the other, on the same reel of film. These records are filled with this type of inconsistency. All I can add is that when dealing with these records, be prepared for the unexpected.

The good news is that these lists are available for the period 1820 to 1954. There are other arrival records that are not covered by the catalog. The bad news is that many years are not indexed at present. Even the years that are indexed are not necessarily helpful. Many passenger manifests contain little more than the name, age, and country of origin of the immigrant. In the early days, only as much information as was required by law was recorded. Like naturalization procedures and vital records, passenger lists went through a similar evolution.

As time passed, more and more information was required and recorded. At some point the steamship companies were held responsible for the return passage of persons rejected by immigration officials. They probably sought recourse for payment of the return fare. How could they accomplish this without some detailed record of who the person was and where he came from?

At least a half dozen people have told me the old wives' tale about a grandfather who successfully stowed away on a passenger ship out of Hamburg, Germany. In each case, the man had gone down to the pier, mingled with the crowd, and then slipped aboard the first boat to America. They never were able to explain how he got off the boat in the middle of New York Harbor, where each passenger went through a check-off list before being boated to Ellis Island to pass through American immigration officials. Aside of the fact that stowaways were treated in the same manner as western horse thieves, it is hard to believe anyone would buy this story. I mention it to point out the thoroughness of record keeping on both sides of the ocean.

The vast majority of immigrants to America passed through two major German ports. They were Bremen and Hamburg. Each had detailed passenger lists of all people who left those ports. The Bremen lists were destroyed by Allied bombing during World War II. However, the Hamburg lists are available and are used daily by people at various branches of the Family History Center at the Latter Day Saints Church. They are indexed and cover the time period from about 1856 to 1934. To find out more about them, I suggest you visit your local Family History Center library before proceeding. By the way, these lists are handwritten in German script.

Many American passenger arrival lists are also indexed. If your ancestors arrived at Philadelphia, the indexed years cover the period from 1800 to 1906. Quite a span. However, if New York was the port of entry, the index covers the years between 1897 and 1943. The first section of this group from June 1897 to June 1902 is filed alphabetically. The second group from July 1902 through December of 1943 is Soundexed. That is the good news. The bad news is that the quality of the film is poor. This applies especially to the index. I have gone through rolls of index film that contained hundreds of blank index cards.

If you have checked the index personally and know that an index card does not exist, all is not lost. Redouble your efforts to locate the person's Declaration of Intention or Petition for Naturalization.

If you can locate either the name of the ship or the date of arrival, it is still possible to check the ship manifest itself. Even if you suspect that your ancestors may have immigrated from the port of Hamburg, it would certainly pay to check the index. In spite of the fact that you must deal with script written in German, checking the lists is not an insurmountable task. Many English names are almost identical in German. There are several good books on the shelves of most libraries that help with this problem.

Even here, the bottom line is that the amount of effort you put in will determine the degree of your success. I sometimes put things aside for lack of results but I seldom give up. There is always another way to approach the problem.

Federal Census Schedules for 1900, 1910 and 1920

	1900	1910	1920
Street and House Number	1900	1910	1920
Relationship to Head of Family	1900	1910	1920
Month and Year of Birth	1900		
Age at Last Birthday	1900	1910	1920
Married or Single	1900	1910	1920
Number of Years Married	1900	1910	1920
Number of Children	1900	1910	
Number of Children Living	1900	1910	
Place of Birth	1900	1910	1920
Birthplace of Father	1900	1910	1920
Birthplace of Mother	1900	1910	1920
Year of Immigration To U.S.	1900	1910	1920
Number of Years in U.S.	1900		
Naturalized or Alien	1900	1910	1920
Trade or Profession	1900	1910	1920
Nature of Business or Industry		1910	1920
Working or Self-Employed		1910	1920
Residence Owned or Rented	1900	1910	1920
Home Owned Free or Mortgaged		1920	

In my opinion, the federal censuses covering the years 1900, 1910, and 1920 are by far the best overall source of information available for most genealogical research during that time. The wealth of information contained in them, and the additional leads they supply, can keep you busy for a long time. There is an additional bonus: Most of the vital records covering that period are readily available.

Because they are somewhat similar in content, the preceding chart points out the years each of the items appears in each census. There are certain things to remember when dealing with census records: The information they contain is not verified in any way. The person taking the census information was instructed to write down the information as it was given to him. He was not there to challenge, dispute, or verify any of the questions that were asked. It was difficult enough to get into the home to record a census, never mind alienating everyone by challenging their answers.

Suppose a wife had lied to her husband about her age. Do you think she was going to admit it to a stranger? Or suppose that the husband had done the same thing. There are many reasons why people lie about age. In most cases, the lie only involved a few years, and mostly it was to make themselves younger. The number of years married was also sometimes slightly exaggerated by a year or so. This was to cover the early arrival of their first child. The reasons are unimportant and really do not hamper research. It only means searching a couple of extra years in a vital records index.

Some of the errors recorded were the result of poor translation and some ignorance. For example, the census taker did not make a habit of asking people who did not speak English to spell their names. He simply wrote down the name the way it sounded to him. When asked the month of birth, many Jewish people went by the Hebrew calendar. The Hebrew month is dictated by the lunar cycle, which is only about twenty-eight days. In converting this to our calendar it was easy to be off a month in either direction. The census taker himself was a temporary employee who would be out of work in a few weeks. Total accuracy was not his top priority. In spite of all these minor problems, I am convinced that they did a fantastic job under the circumstances.

As with the post-1906 naturalization records, these censuses provide leads that have already been discussed in detail. Using them properly can provide leads to all the vital records mentioned, as well as other sources. The proper use of these three census schedules can lead you through more than twenty of the most exciting years in our history. If you choose to pursue the matter historically, there is easily enough material that can be traced through this period to keep you busy for some time. After all these years, I still find myself going back to trace newly found family members.

Social Security Death Index

Last Name and First Name of Person (No Middle Initials Used)
Date of Birth
Social Security Number
State Number Issued
Death Date
Death Residence Localities

This is a relatively new genealogical source that I am sure will become an extremely valuable research tool as soon as more researchers start using it. The entire index consists of four compact discs that you can easily hold in the palm of your hand. They contain the names of more than forty million people who either received Social Security benefits or had families who applied for death benefits when the individual died. This material is most easily accessed via computer at the Family History Center at the Latter Day Saints Church.

Because most of the people in this index were elderly when they passed away, the time span involved here almost always takes us some distance into the past. Personally, I prefer to start in the present by referring to the various *New York Times* indexes. The Obituary Index is the most important. If I can locate an obituary, it generally puts me a short distance away from contact with loving family members who are listed in the obituary. If this fails, I go back to the year of birth and try to locate the individual in the birth certificate index. Even if a common family name is involved it isn't difficult to pinpoint. Remember, this source provides the exact birth date. If this fails I try the city directories to locate the family. There is always another path to take. Just use your imagination. For example, are you aware that even without using this index it is possible to figure out what state a Social Security number was issued in? The first three digits are a code. Here is the breakdown:

Social Security State of Issuance Code

001-003	New Hampshire
004-007	Maine
007-009	Vermont
010-034	Massachusetts
035-039	Rhode Island
040-049	Connecticut
050-134	New York
135-158	New Jersey
159-211	Pennsylvania
212-220	Maryland
221-222	Delaware
223-231	Virginia
232-236	West Virginia
237-246	North Carolina
247-251	South Carolina
252-260	Georgia
261-267	Florida
268-302	Ohio
303-317	Indiana
318-361	Illinois
362-386	Michigan
387-399	Wisconsin
400-407	Kentucky
408-415	Tennessee

416-424	Alabama
425-428	Mississippi
429-432	Arkansas
433-439	Louisiana
440-448	Oklahoma
449-467	Texas
468-477	Minnesota
478-485	Iowa
486-500	Missouri
501-502	North Dakota
503-504	South Dakota
505-508	Nebraska
509-515	Kansas
516-517	Montana
518-519	Idaho
520	Wyoming
521-524	Colorado
525,585	New Mexico
526-527	Arizona
528-529	Utah
530	Nevada
531-539	Washington
540-544	Oregon
545-573	California
574	Alaska
575-576	Hawaii
577-579	District Of Columbia
580	Virgin Islands
581-585	Puerto Rico, Guam American Samoa, Philippine Islands
700-729	Railroad

CHAPTER 9

Computer Genealogy

One of the most common questions asked by newcomers to genealogy is, "When should I start to think about getting a computer?" This question comes up so often that I feel it merits a direct answer, separate from the main body of this book. That is because, in retrospect, I realize that I should have gone to computer years ago. This does not apply to everyone. In my case it was because at various times over the years I felt as though I was "losing it." At times I was convinced that I was developing early symptoms of Alzheimer's disease. I constantly mislaid papers I was working with and couldn't even find names and addresses that I used on a daily basis. In retrospect I realize that I was simply dealing with "acute data overload," a symptom commonly associated with people engaged in heavy genealogical research.

When is the right time for a genealogist to go to computer? How much information should you amass before switching to computer? Am I too old a dog to learn new tricks such as how to use a computer? Is it worth the expense? All of these questions and more come up all the time when talking with people who are even lightly involved in genealogy. I'll try to answer all of them and give my overview of the best method of handling these types of problems. Perhaps I should start by describing how I handled my situation.

When I finally made the decision to go on computer, I had already amassed countless handwritten notes copied from many sources, including city directories, birth, death, and marriage indexes, federal censuses, and numerous other records. These notes were written on everything from cocktail napkins to matchbook covers. Even though I usually knew exactly where everything was, I was never able to come up with any way of cataloging my notes in a file cabinet. The beginning of the problem was so subtle that I was not even aware that anything was wrong. As stated earlier, my problem began at isolated times when I felt as though I was "losing it." It wasn't until things got out of control that I was even aware that any problem existed. When this feeling of "losing it" began to occur with regularity, I realized that the time had come.

When the decision to go on computer was made, I had the advantage of already being computer literate. That is, I understood the basics of computer operation and knew how to input information, as well as how to extract it. This basic knowledge included the ability to set up and use a printer. All of this knowledge can easily be obtained by reading several nontechnical books, such as *PC's for Dummies* and perhaps *DOS for Dummies*. ("PC" stands for Personal Computer and "DOS" is short for Disk Operating System.) Books of this nature should take care of the "old dog learning new tricks" problem. Between them, they cover almost everything you must know to handle the basics of a computer system. They are not books that must be read cover to cover. Instead, they are designed to be referred to when you think you have a problem.

Within thirty days of making my decision to purchase a complete computer system, I had input all the information I had into the computer. What a difference. I still couldn't remember phone numbers or locate names and addresses. However, all the frustration was gone. I knew where the information was. What a relief.

After some looking around, I settled on a bottom of the line set up that consisted of a Leading Edge Model D with keyboard and a monochrome monitor. The total cost was under $200. The system had a 20-megabyte hard drive with a 5 1/4 floppy disk, which supported a random access memory (RAM) of 640 kilobytes. A 20-meg hard drive can handle dozens of programs. The 640K floppy handles all but the newest, most sophisticated software. My system was almost ten years old and would be considered a dinosaur by any normal standard. However, it easily handles everything I want it to do. Two weeks later I purchased a CGA color monitor at a garage sale for $20. The following week I found a Panasonic KX-P 1180 Dot Matrix Printer for $15. A month later I added a Hayes Modem that I purchased for $10. This allowed me to borrow library books or explore library files by computer. For under $250 I was able to put together a system that does everything I want it to do. With a little time and effort anyone can do the same.

There are numerous genealogical programs available. After trying several of them I went with one called Family Origins. I've found it to be the most flexible for my purposes and the easiest to maneuver around in. It is possible to have on screen a five-generation chart all at once. A recent upgrade also computes the complete relationship between people contained in your database. A Windows version also makes it possible to insert scanned photographs of your ancestors into the program. Now that I am all set up, what about you?

What do the newer, more expensive systems do that mine doesn't? Basically there are four things that a newer, costlier model will do that my old system won't:

1. It will have a chip such as a 286, 386, 486 or the latest, the Pentium chip, which will put information on the screen seconds faster than my ancient 8088 chip. It will also compute and change screens faster. The slower speed doesn't bother me a bit.

2. Most newer models come with a mouse-driven program called Windows that allows you to move from place to place by pointing a directional arrow at a small icon or picture. This eliminates having to memorize and use keyboard commands, which require minimal typing skills. Even if you use a mouse and Windows, some typing skill is still needed as your genealogical information still has to be entered by keyboard. (A mouse is a small handheld tool with a marblelike bearing underneath. It is rolled by hand on a small pad and points a directional arrow visible on the screen. When the arrow is in the correct position, you press a button with your finger and this acts the same as a typed-in command.)

3. All new models have superior color graphics and screen resolution that are almost comparable to a fine-tuned TV set. This feature doesn't interest me at all.

4. In my opinion the biggest single objection to going to computer is cost. If money is no object, then rush on down to your local computer store and buy one of their advanced systems. Then be prepared to hire someone to set it up (sometimes the store provides this) and give

you several hours of basic instruction on how to use it. Most new systems usually include Windows and a mouse. However, be sure to remember that when it comes to inputting genealogical data, the information still has to be typed in. The only thing the mouse does is enable you to move around quickly. It doesn't do any typing of information. If cost is a factor and you have no familiarity with systems at all, you can keep costs to a minimum by going to a dealer in used equipment and explaining in detail what you feel your limited needs are. When cutting a deal, make certain that it includes some short-term guarantee on the equipment and several hours of instruction on how to use it.

There are now many additional free services that you can take advantage of with the use of a modem. For example, while sitting at my desk at home I can scan through the catalog of the Library of Congress in Washington. This is done by simply having the computer dial a local number that hooks into the entire Library User's Information Service Network. In Florida this is better known as LUIS. If I choose, I can scan the index of the books on the shelves of most Florida college libraries. I can download most of this information, or simply print a screen of the specific information I want.

There are numerous bulletin boards that computer users can tie into that cater to various Special Interest Groups (SIG). Subjects cover everything from stock market information to genealogy. We have one here in Orlando that is called Cornucopia. It specializes in Jewish Genealogy. Once again, by using a local phone number it is possible to get in touch with hundreds of people who are interested in the same thing. You can ask questions and get answers as well as leave and receive messages. The research possibilities here are almost endless.

There are numerous software programs dealing with a technique commonly called "mail merge." It allows you to write one letter and be able to automatically print an original copy that is personally addressed to as many people as you choose to send it to. This is exactly how my letter to the "Edward Margolins" on my list was handled.

In retrospect I am certain that if I was starting anew today, I would go on computer immediately. I would start on a computer and grow with it. This also circumvents having to learn new tricks. As you amass information and feed it in, it is only necessary to back up the disk in order to protect the data. The bottom line is simple: Computers are here to stay. You may have been around before they were, but there is one real fact you can make book on: They will be around long after you are gone. Happy computing.

Epilogue

People constantly ask me if genealogy has changed my life in any way. You bet! It has not only changed it, but in some ways turned my world upside down. For more than forty years I was a somewhat noncaring, nonpracticing Christian who had no real idea of who I was, or where I was going. Like other people, most of my life had been spent working for a living. This was a trade off that provided me the best lifestyle obtainable in exchange for the talent I had to offer. In retrospect, I realize that the time spent in business during those years contributed nothing to me as a human being. In addition, I was always aware that there was something missing in my life, but I had no idea what the missing element was.

Learning how my ancestors lived and what they accomplished has provided at least part of that missing element and given some new meaning to my life. One of the most important things I discovered was that no matter how rough I thought I had it, my ancestors had things a lot rougher. They had to cross an ocean to get here. When they did, the first thing they had to do was learn a new language. Survival depended upon it. If they happened to be Jewish, they had additional problems. As late as 1937, United States government agencies still classified Jews as members of the Hebrew "race." Perhaps this had something to do with the rampant prejudice they suffered. I now realize that what my father went through growing up as a first-generation American was far tougher than I had ever imagined. The relative degree of their success gives me inspiration, as well as a sense of pride.

None of my relatives came to America on the *Mayflower*, fought in the American Revolution, or participated in the signing of the Declaration of Independence. Yet, I am convinced that each of them, in their own way, made some contribution to the outcome of world history. To Itta Ruchel and Samuel Budiansky, *America* was little more than a word. Perhaps it was their dream for their children. What did Itta Ruchel and Samuel contribute to history? Their grandson, Louis P. Boudin, made a significant contribution as a lawyer and authority on American constitutional law. I now realize that at times it is the descendant who makes the most measurable and recognizable contribution.

In addition to the direct-line relatives mentioned in this book, I have also found dozens of other relatives who had to overcome insurmountable odds just to survive. All of them made their own contribution in some way to the great ledger called "world history." However, discovering this type of tenacity and dedication in my relatives has caused me to rethink some of my values and expectations. I could never obtain this impetus from researching the ancestors of some other person. So you see, my research provided me with another part of the missing element. This was the inner feeling of direct continuity with the past.

I claim no false pride for my ancestors' accomplishments or failures. If anything, I think of what they did from the standpoint of an honored observer. I am in no way trying to cash in on the deeds of my ancestors. My personal thanks and gratitude go out to every one of them. Without them, I wouldn't even be here to write these words. I am a little of each of them.

My search was never meant to be an ego trip. It was done to find out more about myself and who I am. During the past

LOUIS BOUDIN DIES, LABOR LAWYER, 78

Authority on the Constitution Had Served as Chairman of American ORT Unit

Louis B. Boudin, noted labor lawyer and authority on constitutional law, died Thursday night at his home, 200 West Fifty-eighth Street, after a long illness. His age was 78.

He was the senior partner of the law firm of Boudin, Cohn & Glickstein at 1776 Broadway, and had served for many years as chairman of the board of directors of American ORT Federation and as a director of World ORT.

In his legal work, Mr. Boudin represented many A. F. L. and C. I. O. unions in important cases before the courts. He refused, however, to take part in factional fights between the two labor groups, although he fought relentlessly against racketeering and corruption in the trade union movement.

Born in Russia in 1874, Mr. Boudin came to the United States in 1891. He received his master's degree from New York University Law School in 1897 and was admitted to the New York bar the next year. He was admitted to practice before the United States bar in 1919.

Socialist Candidate for Court

Before 1919, Mr. Boudin was a member of the Socialist party. He had been its candidate for chief justice of the Court of Appeals. He also ran for associate justice of the same court and justice of the New York State Supreme Court.

In 1907, Mr. Boudin's book, "The Theoretical System of Karl Marx," was published here, and later the volume was translated into many languages. The book was used in the economics departments of several universities as a standard text on the philosophy of Marxism.

After leaving the Socialist party, Mr. Boudin quit political activities to devote his time to his law practice, writing and numerous charitable and community endeavors. In July, 1946, he flew to France to take part in the first post-war conference of the World ORT Union of Paris.

An outstanding legal victory was won by Mr. Boudin when the United States Supreme Court sustained his view that utility workers were entitled to the protection of the Wagner Act. In 1940, he headed the legal fight on the Attorney General's use of the Anti-Trust Laws against trade unions and successfully defended Local 807, International Brotherhood of Teamsters, before the United States Supreme Court.

Deaths

BOUDIN—Louis B., beloved husband of Dr. Anna Pavitt Boudin; devoted father of Eleanor Osborne-Hill and Vera Cohn; dear brother of Joseph B. Samuel, Sarah Edlin and Mary Flanzer. Services Sunday, June 1, 12:45 P. M., "The Riverside," 76th St. and Amsterdam Ave. Interment private.

BOUDIN—Louis B. American ORT Federation grieves over the loss of its distinguished leader, Chairman of The Board for many years, who piloted ORT's program during its most difficult period of rehabilitating the uprooted and dispossessed. LOUIS Boudin secured for the World ORT movement with matchless devotion, integrity and high intellectual leadership. We shall greatly miss the influence for good of this profound scholar and humanitarian leader.
WILLIAM HABER, President,
American ORT Federation.

BOUDIN—Louis B. We have lost a great friend and distinguished adviser, giant of mind and heart, servant of humanity in pursuit of intellect and deed, incomparable in pursuit of universal truth, DAVID ROSENSTEIN,
President, Ideal Toy Corporation.

BOUDIN—Louis. It is with deep sorrow that we record the passing of an eminent leader of the ORT movement. We extend deepest sympathy to his wife, Dr. Anna Boudin, founder and Past President of Women's American ORT.
Mrs. LUDWIG KAPHAN, National Pres.
Women's American ORT.

BOUDIN—Louis B. The officers and Executive Board of the Hotel Trades Council record with sorrow the passing of a great man, a great lawyer, a brother and a leader in the trade union movement, Louis B. Boudin.
JAY RUBIN, President.
PETER A. MORONEY, Secretary.

Obituary of Louis Boudin from The New York Times.

eighteen years, I have put in longer hours, worked harder, and totally enjoyed doing genealogical research more than anything I have ever done for wages.

What my ancestors did or who they were is of little interest to you. It will not affect your lifestyle one iota. However, I can guarantee you that knowing who your ancestors were and what they did will affect your lifestyle. Please don't make the mistake of trying to cash in on their accomplishments. If anything, try to augment them. Do you remember the man who claimed to be related to King Arthur? The attitude of some genealogical researchers is the same. The common thread is their insatiable lust to take credit for the deeds of their ancestors. I agree with a man who once wrote, "Those who have nothing better to boast about than their illustrious ancestors are like potatoes. The best part of them is under the ground."

At various times, I have wondered if I hadn't opened the proverbial "Pandora's box" for myself by becoming involved in genealogical research. That thought usually occurred when my research wasn't moving along as fast as I thought it should be. Most of the time, I realized that I was engaged in one of the few endeavors in my lifetime that had the effect of totally changing my lifestyle and thinking. By the time you read these words I hope to have uncovered at least part of the remainder of my great-great-grandparents. On the day I have all sixteen of them documented, I expect to start on a new project. On that day I plan to begin the search for my thirty-two great-great-great-grandparents!

Appendix

The following list of books contains everything I feel is necessary to get you started on the path to successful genealogical research. All of these books should be available either at your local library or through inter-library loan no matter where you live in the United States. In the event that you want to buy a copy of any of them, most bookstores now have computer access to all books currently in print. In addition, most bookstore computers will go a step further. They are capable of giving you the names of all books written by an author, as well as the expected publication date of books not yet released.

The first three books listed will cover in some detail all the information necessary to get started on the path to successful genealogical research. The next three combined will provide the names and locations of hundreds of federal, state, county, and local record centers covering all fifty states. Later on when you are ready, the *International Vital Records Handbook* will give you the same comprehensive information for overseas record research. *The New Cambridge Modern History Atlas* will answer most of your questions regarding geographical boundaries, both past and present. Each of the volumes mentioned will provide the same type of support for your needs at whatever point you are at in your research. Remember that this list is only a start. As you progress you will find dozens of other specialized books that will answer your advanced questions.

The genealogy computer programs listed at the end of the book are what I consider to be just a few of the best. There are many others that will do the job. However, like discovering the best method of doing research, you must find the one that will be the best for your individual needs. If one doesn't work to your satisfaction, don't hesitate to try others until you find one that satisfies you. A program called GEDCOM will allow you to transfer all of your data from one program to another. More on GEDCOM later. I have a genuine interest in how well you do and would enjoy hearing from you. If you have a specific question I might be able to answer, I will try to do so. I may be reached at P.O. Box 948194, Maitland, FL 32794-8194. Fax number (407) 834-3037. My E-mail address is Robmarlin@aol.com. (That last dot is the end of the sentence and not to be included in my E-mail Address.)

Suggested Reading and Reference Material

General Genealogy

Finding Your Roots	Jeanne Eddy Dixon
	Ballantine Books
Unpuzzling Your Past	Emily Anne Croom
	Betterway Books
The Genealogist's Companion and Sourcebook	
Beyond the Basics	Emily Anne Croom
	Betterway Books

General Reference

Librarian's Guide to Public Records	BRB Publications
Genealogist's Address Book	Elizabeth Petty Bentley
	Genealogical Publishing

County Courthouse Records	Elizabeth Petty Bentley Genealogical Publishing
Ellis Island Source Book	August C. Bolino
Directory of Historical Organizations In the United States and Canada, 14th Edition	American Association for State and Local History Press
Family Diseases: Are You at Risk?	Myra Vanderpool Gormley
Family Names	J. N. Hook
Genealogical Research in the National Archives	National Archives
Genealogical Research in the New York Metropolitan Area	Jewish Genealogical Society of New York
Locating Your Immigrant Ancestor	James C. and Lila Neagles
American Passenger Arrival Records	Michael Tepper Genealogical Publishing
They Came in Ships	John P. Colletta, Phd. Ancestry Inc.
Researching Public Records	Vincent Parco Citidel Pres
The Map Catalog	Vintage Books
Place Name Changes Since 1900	Adman Room Scarecrow Press
Membership Directory American Cemetery Association	American Cemetery Association
New Cambridge Modern History Atlas	Cambridge University Press
Norton Allen Directory of Steamship Arrivals	Genealogical Publishing
The Source	Arlene Eakles and Johni Cerny
International Vital Records Handbook	Thomas J. Kemp

Jewish Genealogy

Finding Our Fathers Dan Rottenberg
From Generation to Generation Arthur Kurzweil

Jewish Reference

*Complete Dictionary of
English and Hebrew Names* Alfred J. Kolatch

*Dictionary of Jewish Names
and Their History* Benzion C. Kaganoff

*Dictionary of Jewish Surnames
from the Russian Empire* Alexander Beider
Avotaynu Inc.

*Jewish Family Names and
Their Origins* Heinrich and Eva H. Guggenheim

Encyclopedia of Jewish Genealogy Jacob Aronson Inc.

Where Once We Walked Gary Mokotoff and Sallyann
Amdur Sack

*How to Document and Locate
Survivors of the Holocaust* Gary Mokotoff
Avotaynu

Specialized Reference

*Search—A Handbook for
Adoptees and Birth Parents* Jane Askin
Oryx Press

*Lifeline—The Action Guide
to Adoption Search* Virgil L. Klunder
Caradium Publishing

You, Too, Can Find Anyone	Joseph J. Culligan
	Hallmark Press
How to Locate Anyone, Anywhere	Ted Gunderson
	E. P. Dutton

Genealogical Computer Programs

The genealogical programs listed here are ones that I have worked with or that I have received positive feedback on from friends. I have not included any prices for several reasons. Costs change every time a program is updated. The updated program usually costs more, while the older version goes on sale. In many cases the older version will serve your purpose. Most larger shopping malls usually have two or three software stores. Shop around before buying as prices fluctuate from store to store.

All of these programs listed have a GEDCOM feature. GEDCOM is an acronym for Genealogical Data Communication. It is a program that allows a standard method of data transfer between different computer programs. This means that you can easily change programs if you aren't happy with the one you are using. This is accomplished by simply exporting all of your data out of the old program and importing it into the new program. It also means that you can share information with other family members or fellow genealogists who may be working on the same family lines. You can simply export the files you wish to share onto a disk and mail it to the person you wish to share the information with. In most cases this feature is included with the program. However, a few software manufacturers charge an extra fee. In any case, I consider it an absolute necessity.

Brother's Keeper

Produced By: John Steed
                                      6907 Childsdate Road
                                      Rockford, MI 49341
                                      (616) 866-9422

This is a shareware program that is available in any computer shop that sells shareware at a minimal cost, or may even be downloaded from many computer bulletin boards free of charge. The idea behind shareware is to allow you to test a program without having to buy it outright. If you are happy with the software, you are expected to pay a registration fee that covers the full cost and includes a printed manual. Mr. Steed is extremely cordial and supplies software support by telephone. A standard GEDCOM feature is included. This program produces superior printed charts. Many genealogists use this as a secondary program because of this outstanding feature. This is another use for the GEDCOM feature.

Family Origins

Produced by: Parson's Technology
                                      One Parsons Drive
                                      P.O. Box 100
                                      Hiawatha, Iowa 52233-0100

This is my favorite. It is easy to use and serves all of my needs. It is available in both DOS and Windows versions. The Windows version even allows you to insert your family photographs into the video display. The first screen display after opening is a three-generation ancestral chart showing all database entries back to your grandparents. A keystroke allows you to zoom in to a five-generation chart that includes space for all sixteen of your great-great-grandparents. This full display never fails to impress me.

Family Tree Maker

Produced By: Banner Blue Software
                                P.O. Box 7865
                                Fremont, CA 94537
                                (510) 794-6850

This publisher claims that their program is designed for the hobbyist and I believe their claims to be true. The program is also available in both DOS and Windows versions. In addition, the DeLuxe Edition has a CD-ROM listing more than one hundred million names found in various American records. This includes state and federal records that include the Social Security Death Index. However, the only information supplied is the location of each record. In order to access what is in that record, it is necessary to buy or have access to additional CD-ROM material. Naturally, Banner Blue produces CD-ROMs for most of these record sources.

Personal Ancestral File

Produced By: Church of Jesus Christ of Latter Day Saints
                  Family History Department
                  Ancestral File Operations Unit 2WW
                  50 E. North Temple Street
                  Salt Lake City, UT 84150

This program is produced by the Mormon Church and is especially helpful to those who do research there. It is available in DOS and Macintosh versions. This program is fairly easy to use, but the various features and the way they are used may appear to be complex. A comprehensive manual is included that explains each feature in some detail.

Roots IV

Produced By:　　　　　　　　Commsoft Inc.
　　　　　　　　　　　　　　7795 Bell Road
　　　　　　　　　　　　　　P.O. Box 310
　　　　　　　　　　　　　　Windsor, CA 95492-6687
　　　　　　　　　　　　　　(800) 327-6687

Considered by many researchers to be the cremè de la cremè of genealogical programs. It has won a number of awards, which are merited. In my opinion it is far too complex for my needs, or the needs of all but the die-hard researcher. It is complex, takes time to learn, and is not recommended for beginners. Commsoft will send you a free sample disk that will allow you to judge for yourself.

A very satisfying experience will occur on the day that you enter your research data into a computer and then call it up on the screen. Seeing your family history scrolling before your eyes may bring a few tears. It is also instant reward for the countless hours spent gathering the information. The ability to print out and share all this information usually creates much pleasure.

Index

American Genealogical Lending Library, 154

Ancestor chart, 52, 106, 169

"Aunt Jenny." *See* Cherson, Aunt Jenny

Auerbach, Leslie (Margolin), 12, 161-168

Berkowsky, Edward, 138

Berkowsky, Isaac, 140

Berkowsky, Joseph, 138

Berkowsky, Nathan, 138, 139

Berkowsky, Rose (Resnick), 138, 144

Bernhard family, 184

Bernhard, Lena. *See* Kruse, Lena (Bernhard)

Bernhard, Sarah, 58

Bikoff family, 135

Birth certificate, 30, 36, 37, 41, 173-176

    index, 59, 175, 187

Boston Public Library, 84

Boudin, Katie, 73

Boudin, Leonard, 99

Boudin, Louis P. B., 73, 125, 214

Boudin, Peter, 69, 71, 73, 74, 129, 131, 135

Brooklyn *Eagle,* 62

Boudiansky. *See* Budiansky

Budiansky family, 134, 135, 137

Budiansky, Itta Ruchel (Cohen), 135, 137, 144, 214

Budiansky, Pessie (Pesha) (Boudiansky), 20, 73, 108, 132, 135, 136

Budiansky, Samuel, 134, 144, 214

Budiansky, Sarah (Bodjansky), 151, 152

Budinoff, Louis, 145, 147

Budinoff, Max, 147

Budinoff, Rabbi Meyer (Boudiansky), 73, 129, 131, 142, 148

Budinoff, Pearl, 145

Budinoff, Rachael (Rebecca) (Slutsky), 132, 145, 147

Budinoff, Ruth, 147

Budinoff, Samuel L., 131, 132, 197

Budinsky, Raisel. *See* Resnick, Rose (Raizel)

Cemeteries, as sources, 182-183

Census, 79-82, 110, 113-114,

    index, 79, 81

    New York State, 117, 155

    sans Soundex, 110-113

    schedules, 201

    United States (Federal), 48, 79, 173

    United States-1790, 79

    United States-1850, 159

    United States-1860, 79, 159

United States-1870, 159
United States-1880, 80
United States-1890, 79
United States-1900, 79, 80, 105,
    108, 113, 114, 132, 201
United States-1910, 79, 105, 108,
    110, 111, 117, 201
United States-1920, 79, 108, 111,
    114, 138, 153, 201
Cherson, Aunt Jenny, 66-69, 71, 74
Church of Jesus of Latter Day Saints.
    See Family History Center
Coyne, Beckie, 137, 150
Coyne, family, 136
Crawford, Eleanor, 11

Death certificate, 19, 30, 36, 37, 39,
    40, 97, 179-181
    index, 19, 98
    New York City death index, 57
Declaration of Intention, 124, 125,
    129, 182, 187-191
Directories, city, 16, 37, 38, 84, 102,
    138, 172, 175, 178, 181, 184-
    187
    Polk, R. L. & Co., 38
    telephone, 16, 38, 133, 185
Disraeli, Benjamin, 47
divorce, Jewish (git), 162

Ellenoff, Rae, 134
Enumeration districts, 110-113, 159
    indexes, 114

Family History Center (L.D.S.
    Church), 11, 50, 73, 114, 117,
    138, 139, 199, 203
Ford, Henry, 26
Frank, Hilda (Margolin), 56

Genealogical chart. See Ancestor
    chart
Genetic diseases, 29, 183
Genetic makeup, 28
Great Neck Library (L.I.), 18

Halloran, Clara, 32, 33
Herring, Nathan, 184
Herring, Sarah. See Korris, Sarah
    (Herring)
Holocaust, 26

Immigration list. See Passenger arrival
    records
Immigration and Naturalization Ser-
    vice, U.S. Department of, 124,
    188
Interview, oral, 33, 67-69, 77

Jewish Genealogical Society of
    Greater Orlando, 10
Jewish burial society. See United
    Friends and Relatives
Johnson, John, 32
Johnson, Lena (Kruse), 32, 94, 97,
    98, 160
Johnson, Margaret, 97
Johnson, William, 97

Katz, Bertha (Margolin), 117, 153,
    155, 163
Katz family, 154, 155
Katz, Lillie, 155
Katz, Samuel, 117, 153, 155, 163,
Katz, Sarah, 155
Katz, Sylvia, 153
Keller, John, 92
Keller, Marie. See Wild, Maria (Keller)
Koris. See Korris
Korris & Herring, 184

Korris, Abraham (Abe), 56, 69, 113, 116, 117, 188

Korris, Bella. *See* Sachar, Bella (Korris)

Korris family, 184, 185

Korris, Gertrude, 185

Korris, Hyman (Chiam Kuraris), 20, 56, 57, 65, 69, 73, 108, 184

Korris, Meyer, 56, 69, 184, 185

Korris, Rose (Siegel), 68, 71, 108, 119, 131

Korris, Sarah (Herring), 184

Korris, William, 65, 69

Kouter, Celie, 140-141

Kranz, Temma, 20, 168

Kruger, Mary B.(Kruse), 97

Kruger, Catherine (Kruse), 97

Kruse, Katherine (Wild), 32, 77-79, 85

Kruse family, 32, 57, 59, 77, 94, 97, 102, 158, 159, 173, 184

Kruse, Florence Helena, 32

Kruse, Frederick (Fred), 32, 97, 101, 102, 158

Kruse, Georgetta, 33

Kruse, Honos. *See* Kruse, Louis C.

Kruse, John Patrick, 32, 33, 58, 59, 62, 94, 102, 158

Kruse, John Jr., 32, 57

Kruse, Kenneth, 33, 35, 57, 59

Kruse, Lena (Bernhard), 58, 62, 94, 96, 97, 102, 158, 160, 168

Kruse, Lizzie, 94, 160

Kruse, Louis Christian, 35, 57-59, 62, 94, 96, 97, 102, 158, 160, 168

Kruse, Louis (son of Louis C.), 97

Kruse, Marian, 32

Kuraris, Bella, 69

Kuraris, Beckie, 108

Kuraris, Chaim. *See* Korris, Hyman

Kuraris, Rose. *See* Korris, Rose (Siegel)

Lerner family, 136, 148

Levinson, Jacob, 53, 56

Levy, Roshi (Rose), 65

Lutheran Cemetery (Queens, N.Y.), 59, 94

Maiden name, 39, 175, 178

Margolin, Bessie, 155, 167

Margolin, Bertha. *See* Katz, Bertha (Margolin)

Margolin, Edward, 155, 157, 161, 166

Margolin, Mrs. Edward, 161

Margolin family, 36, 184

Margolin, Harry, 117-119, 121, 153, 155, 162-166, 168, 198

Margolin, Hilda (Korris), 18, 25, 56, 57, 68, 69, 105, 108, 110, 117, 119, 125, 129, 162, 166, 184, 197

Margolin, Hirsch, 20, 117, 168

Margolin, Meyer, 19, 20, 24, 56, 68, 73, 105, 108, 110, 117, 124, 125, 162-166, 184

Margolin, Paul, 16, 18, 56, 119, 121, 168

Margolin, Rose (Rubin), 162

Margolin, Ruth, 18, 121

Margolin, Samuel, 18, 68, 69, 119, 121, 168

Margolin, Ted, 121, 122, 123, 166, 167

Margolin, William, 18, 56, 168

Marriage (license) certificate, 20, 30, 37-39, 176-179

index, 40, 73, 139, 148, 150, 158, 160, 178

Mayflower, 214

Melnick, David, 99, 137, 150, 151

Melnick family, 135, 137, 149
Melnick, Hyman, 151
Montefiore Cemetery, 20, 21, 53, 144
Myerson, Vivian, 11, 66-69
National Archives (Federal), 145, 166, 197
    Bayonne, NJ, 110, 124
    Boston, MA, 85
    form NATF, 119
    Passenger Arrival Records Division, 118
Naturalization papers, 85, 124,
    Post-1906, 194-197
    Pre-1906, 124, 187, 192-195
New York Public Library, 16, 19, 59
New York Times, indexes,
    General Index, 98, 100
    Obituary Index, 98-100, 102, 138, 149-150, 203
    Personal Surname Index, 98, 100
Noordland, S. S., 69

Orange County Library System, 114
Orlando Public Library, 11, 43, 45, 116, 155
Passenger arrival records, 40, 140, 172, 182, 197-200
Passenger list (manifest), 80, 118, 119, 140, 154, 198-200

Patents,
    combination furniture, 59
    wax crayon, 56
Petition for Naturalization, 124, 125, 129, 182, 188
Pogrom, in Russia, 162
Polk, R. L. & Company. See Directories
Pretoria, S. S., 162, 166, 198

Rachlin, Nathan, Dr., 152

Research etiquette, 42-49
Resnick, Abe, 136
Resnick, David, 136
Resnick family, 136, 138, 144
Resnick, Ida, 136
Resnick, Meyer, 140
Resnick, Pauline, 136
Resnick, Rose (Raizel) (Budiansky), 135, 136, 138, 140, 143, 144
Resnick, Ruth, 12, 134, 136, 137, 148, 152
Rubin, Rose. See Margolin, Rose (Rubin)

Sachar, Anne, 56, 65
Sachar, Bella (Korris), 53, 56, 66, 131, 197
Sachar family, 71
Sachar, Meyer, 56, 66
Sachar, Willie, 53, 56, 57
Schlossberg, Eva, 155
Schlossberg, William, 155
Schlossberg, Winifred, 155
Schor, Rebecca (Budiansky), 144
Sickle Cell Anemia, 29
Siegel, David (father of Ike), 73
Siegel family, 71, 74
Siegel, Isaac W. (Ike Siegel) (Isaac Segal), 68, 71, 73, 125, 129, 131, 141, 143
Siegel, Jennie, 150, 151
Siegel, Meyer, 68, 74
Siegelman, Bernard (Siegal), 74, 141
Siegelman, David, 74
Siegelman family, 74
Siegelman, Gitel (Katie), 74
Siegelman, Isaac, 74
Siegelman, Meyer, 74
Sloat, Ben, (Slutsky), 136
Slutsky, Anne, 147
Slutsky, Benjamin, 147, 148

Slutsky, Bertha, 137, 152
Slutsky family, 135, 137, 144
Slutsky, Joseph, 147, 148
Slutsky, Shaya (Simon), 137, 144, 152
Slutsky, William, 147
Social Security Death Index, 50, 74, 172, 203
Social Security State of Issuance Code, 204-205
Soultz, France, 85, 140
Souls [sic] France. See Soultz
Soundex, 79, 94, 105, 110, 124, 138, 155, 200
    code, 48, 80, 94, 105, 124
    index, 80-81,
Summerfield, David, 99, 108, 132
Summerfield, Libby (Boudinoff), 108, 132, 134, 135, 137
Summerfield, Pauline, 108
Summerfield Rachael, 108
Sunshine family, 136
Sunshine, Florence, 137
Sunshine, Jennie (Melnick), 137, 150
Surname, 14, 26, 27, 39, 44, 48, 175

Tay-Sachs disease, 29
Telephone books. See Directories

Ten Commandments of Genealogical Research, 46

United Friends and Relatives, 22, 53, 65, 132
Unrelated miscellaneous documents file, 145

Vital records, 37, 172
Voltaire (Francois Marie Arouet), 26

Ward, political subdivision, 62, 159
Wendel, Catherine (Wenoel), 89
Wild family, 32, 81, 82, 94, 139, 184
Wild, Frank, 78
Wild, George, 78
Wild, John, 78
Wild, Joseph, 78
Wild, Louisia, 78
Wild, Mary, 78
Wild, Maria, 77-79, 82, 85, 90, 139, 140, 168
Wild, Matthias, 35, 77-79, 82, 85, 90, 139, 140, 168
Wild, Peter, 89

Zeeland, S. S., 69

To order additional copies of *My Sixteen*:

By Mail: Send check, money order, or credit card information (Visa and MasterCard only) to Land Yacht Press, P.O. Box 210262, Nashville, TN 37221. For ease of use, please use order form below.

By Fax: Fax your order with credit card information (Visa and MasterCard only) to 615-646-2086, 8 AM to 6 PM CST, 7 days a week.

Multiple copies: To order multiple copies for resale write or fax for wholesale information.

****

Order form:

Name: _____

Address: _____

City:_____State:_____ZIP _____

Daytime Phone: (____) _____

Credit card number: _____ Exp. Date: _____

Visa_____ Master Card_____ Signature _____

Number of copies_____ x $14.95
plus $3.00 shipping/handling;
  (.50 for each additional book)
Tennessee residents add 8.25% sales tax;
Total enclosed:_____

Mail To:

Land Yacht Press
Order Department
P.O. Box 210262
Nashville, TN 37221